The Art
of the
Automobile

The Art of the Automobile

THE 100 GREATEST CARS

Written and Photographed
by Dennis Adler

HarperResource

An imprint of HarperCollinsPublishers

HarperCollins books may be purchased for educational, business, or sales promotional use. For information please write:
Special Markets Department, HarperCollins Publishers Inc., 10 East 53rd Street, New York, NY 10022–5299.
Printed in China
FIRST EDITION
Designed by Pisaza Design Studio, Ltd.

ISBN 0-06-105128-4

Visit HarperCollins on the World Wide Web at http://www.harpercollins.com

99 00 01 02 03 10 9 8 7 6 5 4 3 2 1

DEDICATION

To Barry & Karen Meguiar
for their support and belief in this book,
To my darling Jeanne, who will
always be number one in my book,
And to Jay Leno and Bruce Meyer
for their friendship and selfless devotion
to the collector car hobby

TABLE OF CONTENTS

—◁○▷—

—◁○▷—

A CENTURY OF CARING FOR THE WORLD'S GREATEST CARS

When Dennis Adler asked us if we would like to work with him to present this volume of the 100 greatest cars, we jumped at the opportunity. With the approach of our own 100th anniversary, we were already looking for a way to celebrate the cars that have fueled the passion of our family business these many years.

Since 1901, four generations of my family have been car enthusiasts with an obsession for making great cars look absolutely perfect. And through the years, we have shared their owners' exhilaration when they have won Best of Class and Best of Show honors at the major collector car events around the world. For our family and our corporate team, this is the payoff.

For our first 70 years, Meguiar's Mirror Glaze polishes and waxes were only formulated for use in assembly plants, car dealerships, body shops, restoration shops (what we now call detailers), and serious car enthusiasts. And until 1970, our home was Pasadena, California, which was also home to the Walter M. Murphy Company, and later Bohman & Schwartz—two of the greatest coachbuilders of the classic era.

Back in the Twenties and Thirties, one would order the bare chassis and drivetrain from a car manufacturer and then have a coachbuilder, such as Murphy, create the body . . . quite a few of which were custom, one-off designs built for stars of the stage and screen, heads of state, and captains of industry—anyone from the president of the United States to a tenor with the Metropolitan Opera to the heiress to a candy company. Many of those same cars are recognized in these pages as being among the 100 greatest cars of all time. And very often they have been polished with our products ever since they were first produced more than 70 years ago. This has been our life.

The rising demand for our polishes and waxes eventually forced us to make them more readily available. This is why we created what has become our top-selling line of "Meguiar's" car care products, which are now sold to the public through retailers everywhere. Nevertheless, we have continued to devote our primary resources to supporting and building the collector car hobby. And we have continued to focus on making the greatest cars ever built look their impeccable best.

This is our passion, and this book is a tribute to the greatest of the great.

—*Barry Meguiar*

since 1901

1970's-Present

1940's-1960's

1930's

1920's

ACKNOWLEDGMENTS

An author is like a conductor, and without musicians there isn't much of an orchestra! To create a book of this magnitude requires the efforts of many people—car collectors, museum curators, restorers, historians, and a raft of individuals working behind the scenes to make things happen. It is a cooperative effort, and while I may have written the words and taken the photographs, it could not have been done without the help of many others, including my close associates T. C. Browne, Frank Barrett, and Westley Peterson.

The majority of automobiles featured in *The Art of the Automobile* come from the finest car collections in the United States: the Nethercutt Collection, the Otis Chandler Vintage Museum of Transportation & Wildlife, the Robert M. Lee Collection, the Jerry J. Moore Collection, the Dr. Joseph A. Murphy Collection, the Blackhawk Collection, the Jay Leno Collection, the Sam and Emily Mann Collection, the Bruce Meyer Collection, the John McMullen Collection, the Arturo Keller Collection, and the collections of Jim Hull, Peter Mullin, David Sydorick, Chip Miller, Jack Dunning, Noel Thompson, Jerry McAlevy, William B. Ruger, Sr. and Jr., and Tom Reddington. Without the help of these fine collectors and their devotion to the preservation of the world's greatest automobiles, this book could never have been possible.

I would like to extend special thanks to the Meguiar family for their support and belief in this project and its importance to the collector car hobby, and to my agent, Peter Riva, for never giving up on this book, even when it appeared that others had. Our thanks and appreciation also go out to the many homeowners in the cities of Pasadena, Beverly Hills, Fillmore, and Santa Paula, California, who opened their doors to us to provide historic backdrops for so many of the photographs in this book. Additional locations were provided courtesy of historic Meadow Brook Hall and Oakland University in Rochester, Michigan, Mr. John McMullen, Planet Hollywood, Universal Studios Hollywood, Mr. Jerry J. Moore, and the Los Angeles City Department of Parks and Recreation.

These are the musicians in the orchestra, and this humble conductor gives his thanks and appreciation to each of them for their contributions.

—*Dennis Adler*

BY JAY LENO

There have been so many achievements in automotive design and engineering since the late 1880s that it seems almost impossible to select only 100 cars to represent more than a century of automobile evolution. That's less than 10 cars per decade! Still, there are many that stand head and shoulders above the rest, and recognizing the cars that were the best of their time in their time has always been a welcomed challenge, as well as a fun pastime.

For me, engineering has always been the most important feature of an automobile. Not that I am particularly mechanically inclined, but I've come to respect the accomplishments of great engineers like Walter Owen Bentley, Fred Duesenberg, Harry Miller, Marc Birkigt, Frederick Lanchester, and Ferdinand Porsche—men who stand out because they started with a clean sheet of paper and set the standards others would follow.

This almost becomes a book about the 100 greatest engineers, because the cars they created pioneered the technology that future generations would build upon. Almost everything we consider modern today, such as overhead camshafts, four- and five-valve heads, and the use of lightweight alloys, existed within the first quarter-century of the automobile.

Men such as Duesenberg, Birkigt, and Bentley, and those who followed in their footsteps, improved the performance and quality of the motorcar for nearly a century, and the makes and models that have been touched by these legendary figures—cars like the Model J Duesenberg, Bentley Speed Six, Hispano-Suiza J12, and Mercer Raceabout—have in turn become legendary.

Combing through the pages of automotive history to determine which 100 cars best represent the highest achievements in engineering, design, and styling is no easy task, and I'm glad Dennis is doing it instead of me. It's a bit like making a list of the 100 most beautiful women in the world and then having to explain to your family why your mother, wife, and daughter are not on it. Politics!

Dennis Adler has spent the better part of his career developing a wealth of information and photographs upon which to base the selections featured in *The 100 Greatest Cars*. I've known Dennis for almost 15 years, and he's photographed many of my

own cars during that time. I think his insight into what makes a car great, combined with an eye for the very best coachwork, has been a fundamental element in all of his past books. The cars photographed by Dennis for this book are without question among the most beautiful automobiles ever produced. Many of them were hand-built, one-of-a-kind, custom-produced for film stars, captains of industry, and heads of state. But they do not necessarily eclipse the social importance of cars like the Model T Ford, the Model A, or the original Volkswagen, cars that were built by the millions and have become historical benchmarks in their own right.

As we embark upon a new century, a new millennium, it is perhaps time to reflect upon the miraculous accomplishments that have been made in the last 100 years. How far we've come from the days when breaking a mile a minute was considered impossible. Today sports cars, and even luxury sedans, are capable of speeds once thought only attainable by Indianapolis race cars. Within the pages of this book are 100 cars that take us from the dawning of the auto industry to the threshold of a new century. It's a story that took many lifetimes to create, and one every automotive enthusiast will enjoy reading.

INTRODUCTION

BY DENNIS ADLER

There are great cars, and then there are the truly great cars, those that have not only withstood the test of time but steadfastly defied it—cars that have remained desirable and valuable for more than 50 years, to become the most treasured automotive artifacts of our time.

Many of the automobiles pictured in this book are here because they are stunning examples of the motorcar and require no further credentials. Others have been selected because they were benchmarks in the history of the automobile in this century—the 1948 Porsche Gmünd Limousine, for example, the car that laid the foundation for the future of Porsche.

With the better part of this century behind them, it's safe to say that the majority of rare American and European motorcars featured in *The Art of the Automobile* have become virtually irreplaceable, and that the longer they survive, the more collectable and valuable they will become. However, while rarity and attrition may be the basis for determining what is and is not collectable, the true deciding factor is desirability, best summed up by nineteenth-century author Margaret Wolfe Hungerford, who wrote the prophetic words "Beauty is in the eye of the beholder."

With an automobile, this is a quality far more difficult to define. The pretentious styling of a 1930s Delage or Delahaye bodied by Jacques Saoutchik or Joseph Figoni is as likely to turn stomachs as heads. And while some people are enamored by the towering 1959 Cadillac tail fin, others find it vulgar, an expression of the wretched excess that proliferated throughout an entire decade in America. Therefore, choosing 100 cars to represent the greatest eras in the history of the automobile is a formidable responsibility, but one we gladly undertake in the hope that the controversy sure to follow will incite even greater soul-searching among automotive enthusiasts.

Within the collector car world there are certain marques that are a given, cars that have always seemed larger than life.

"There is a clear separation between the great versus the almost great," claims world-renowned collector car authority Don Williams of the Blackhawk Collection in Danville, California. "This has always been true. The same cars that are the most desirable today are the very same that appealed to early collectors like D. Cameron Peck, George Waterman, Kirk Gibson, and Bill Harrah. No matter how much time passes, these will always be the greatest cars ever built." Collectors refer to them today as "the great cars." They were built in very limited quantities—usually less than 50, sometimes as few as a half-dozen, and occasionally only a single example.

When you talk about modern automobile production, which runs in the millions, the very notion of building 50 cars is almost beyond comprehension, yet that is exactly what makes antique, classic, and early postwar automobiles so intriguing. The temerity of a company producing only a handful, or a single example, of its product seems to fly in the face of reason, adding yet another irresistible dimension to these legendary motorcars.

How do you pick 100 cars out of the thousands of makes and models that have come down the road in the last 100 years? Perhaps the best way to answer that is with another question: "What defines *great*?"

Ask an antique car collector, and the answer will be *technology*. Ask Jay Leno, and he'll be the first to mention the Mercer Raceabout—a car that was at the forefront of automotive technology in the early 1900s. Of course, Jay will also heap laurels on his '09 Stanley Steamer—another superb turn-of-the-century motorcar, and any of his 1930s-era Model J Duesenbergs for *their* particular technological benchmarks.

Broad-minded collectors who own a variety of cars from antiques and classics to postwar big steel, muscle cars and early Ferraris, Lamborghinis, and Porsches usually have a bias toward models that represented the best cars of their time in their time. Every automobile selected for the top 100 was chosen for its exceptional styling, its advanced engineering, or its influence on the automotive world. How else could a Volkswagen Beetle be on the same list as a Model J Duesenberg!

The truth is that there are more great cars behind us than there are ahead. The majority of cars chosen were built before 1950, and one need only glance back at the first half of the twentieth century to realize that the greatest advances in engineering and design occurred between the turn of the century and the beginning of World War II. The balance of essential cars come from the 1950s, when America rediscovered the automobile, the 1960s, when America rediscovered itself, and the early 1970s, when we discovered that bigger isn't better, especially when there isn't any gasoline.

This is not to say that there haven't been some wonderful automobiles built in the past 30 years. In fact, some remarkable cars have been introduced in just the last few years, such as the Ferrari 550 Maranello, the Jaguar XK–8, and the Dodge Viper GTS, but they have yet to prove themselves in the greatest test of all, the test of time.

To make the final selection of cars, opinions gathered from many of the world's leading car collectors formed the basis for a primary list containing 200 automobiles. The second 100 are listed in the appendix, and each was a worthy contender.

Among the leading authorities consulted over the past several years were former General Motors vice president and director of design David Holls, renowned car collectors Otis Chandler, Sam Mann, Robert M. Lee, Jay Leno, Jerry J. Moore, William B. Ruger, Jr., Bruce Meyer, Noel Thompson, Gene Epstein, and Don Williams, Nethercutt Collection president Dick Nolind and collection curator Skip Marketti, retired Ford Motor Company vice president of corporate design Jack Telnack, retired General Motors vice president of design Chuck Jordan, and the man who helped put Chrysler design at the forefront of American automotive styling, DaimlerChrysler executive vice president Tom Gale. Their opinions covering different eras and historically significant cars formed the criteria for establishing not only the final list of 100 cars, but the top 10 cars of the twentieth century.

The old adage that you can't please everyone is perhaps the greatest subtext of this book. The Edsel is not here, nor is the Corvair, or the Kaiser Manhattan. Some will say that there are too many classic and antique cars, too few postwar cars. Why so many Ferraris, Duesenbergs, and Packards? In some instances there is more than one model from a single manufacturer, in which case body style, coachbuilder, or engineering was a determining factor. This is especially true of the Duesenbergs, which are individual cars in their own right, sharing only a common chassis, engine, and name.

Consultant Sam Mann, who has won top honors over the years at both the prestigious Pebble Beach and Meadow Brook Concours d'Elegance, selected both American and European classics. Trained as a designer, he explains that his criterion is "design first, more than anything else. I'm attracted to models that have a lot of design detail. I have no problem finding that same allure in a 1959 Cadillac Eldorado, a 1957 Corvette, or a 1930 Duesenberg Boattail Speedster."

The greatest cars, says Mann, were fast and exciting, "like the Auburn 851 Boattail Speedster, the Cord 812 SC, the Model J and SJ Duesenberg—all cars with stunning coachwork and powerful engines." Of course, Mann also favored early Ferrari sports cars and the Jaguar XK–120. "The great thing about America," he says, "is that taste levels and enthusiasm are all across the spectrum."

Retired General Motors director of design Dave Holls, a classic car collector and cofounder of the Meadow Brook Concours d'Elegance, favored the Mercer Raceabout as one of the all-time great cars, as did well-known Southern California car collectors Bruce Meyer and Jay Leno. "The Mercer was the epitome of a dashing car in the early years," said Holls of the sporty Raceabout. Our entire panel also chose the Model J Duesenberg, "the most spectacular automobile ever to be marketed in production. Price, speed, style, luxury, the Duesenberg had it all," trumpets Holls.

Another 1930s-era classic that most everyone said they would like to own (and a few of them do) is the Mercedes-Benz 540K. "The boldest car of its era," notes one collector. "A true benchmark in Daimler-Benz history," says Williams. Indeed, a 540K is the centerpiece of more than a few great car collections.

Another defining characteristic of greatness is style, that palpable sense of line and proportion so pleasing to the eye that no further considerations need be given. To inspire such profound and irrational emotions, one need look no further than Paris, France, and the *carrosserie* of Joseph Figoni, Jacques Soautchik, the Franay Brothers, Jean-Henri Labourdette, Henri Chapron, and Letourneur et Marchand.

Two models that our panel favored in majority, the Delage D8 120 Aerodynamic Coupé by Letourneur et Marchand, and the Talbot-Lago T150 SS Figoni Teardrop Coupé, are the embodiment of what makes a legendary car. Both were inspired by the aerodynamic vogue that swept the automotive world in the late 1930s, which defined the motorcar as an objet d'art like no other time in automotive history. While neither car was a mechanical marvel, few could match the sheer beauty of these magnificent French marques, making their selection a triumph of styling over substance.

"These cars are in a class of their own," says the Blackhawk Collection's Don Williams. "When you talk about Delages, Delahayes, and Bugattis, among European marques, they have become more than automobiles, they have indeed become collectable art. Let's face it, there are thousands and thousands of different models that have been produced over the years, and only occasionally does something so incredible come along."

No list of the world's greatest cars could stand without Packards, and better than half of our panel favored the Packard Twelve chassis circa 1930–34, fitted with either LeBaron or Dietrich coachwork—what Dave Holls considers "the finest American example of a high-style custom-built automobile."

Packard Twelves were among the most reliable engines on the American road in the 1930s, and even today collectors praise their durability and quality. Couple that with Packard's superb chassis engineering, spellbinding history, and coachwork by the leading designers of the era, and you have the reason so many Packards made the top 100 list.

One will also find the name Hispano-Suiza prominently spelled out on every list of the world's greatest cars. For those who seek the rarest of automobiles, an Hispano-Suiza H6B or J12 ranks among the most coveted of classics. Both models found their way into the final 100.

The Type 57 Bugatti is another that cannot be denied its due, particularly the supercharged Type 57C and SC version. Bred from Bugatti's racing heritage but refined for the open road, the stylish Type 57 chassis, fitted with a variety of coachwork from roadsters to sedans, competed against Delage, Delahaye, and Hispano-Suiza for a share of the luxury sports touring market, a niche that Bugatti nearly dominated throughout the 1930s. The 200-horsepower supercharged Bugattis are among the rarest and most desirable cars in the world. Legendary automotive historian Griff Borgesson once described them as "being possessed of a personality which, for better or worse, was without equal in all of automotive history."

Not surprisingly, postwar sports cars took a fair share of the top 100 spots, and the last two places in the 10 best list went to the Ferrari 250 GTO and Mercedes-Benz 300SL Gullwing Coupe. Both evolved from factory-sponsored racing programs, the 300SL most notably being an off-the-shelf competition car based almost entirely on production car components—the 300 series engine, driveline, suspension, and brakes fitted to a custom-built tubular steel chassis with an alloy and steel body unique in all the world. It is the most recognized sports car ever created, and total production was limited to only 1,400 from 1954 to 1957.

The rarest and most desirable Ferrari road car ever produced was the 250 GTO. Introduced in 1962, this became the quintessential road/race car of the era. The bodies were produced for Ferrari by Scaglietti, and a total of only 39 were built through 1964. Essentially a refined 250 GT short-wheelbase Berlinetta, the cars were equipped with a modified 250 GT engine, Ferrari's most successful V-12, developing a chest-swelling output of 300 horsepower, surrounded by what is arguably the most exciting and most emulated body design of all time.

While there are dozens of cars with suitable provenance to warrant the 10 best list, these are the makes and models most often discussed whenever collectors and automotive historians get together. Greatness, of course, is still a matter of opinion. But few will argue that the 10 marques we have chosen are worthy of leading our list of the 100 greatest cars.

1. Model J Duesenberg

Every list ever compiled in the past 20 years has featured a Duesenberg model. The most famous American car of the classic era, there are more $1 million Duesenbergs than almost any other marque.

2. Mercedes-Benz 540K

3. Packard Twelve

In 1931 the celebrated Spanish firm of Hispano-Suiza entered the multicylinder wars of the classic era by doubling the capacity of its legendary six-cylinder engines, creating the most expensive car in the organization's history: the J–12. A J–12 was capable of reaching a top speed in excess of 110 mph and could clip the distance from 0 to 60 mph in just 12 seconds! Only 100 J–12s were produced, making this not only one of the fastest cars of its time, but also one of the rarest.

4. Hispano-Suiza J 12

5. Bugatti Type 57SC

6. Talbot-Lago T150 SS Teardrop Coupé

There is nothing quite so handsome as a French car from the 1930s. This Delage D8 120 Aerodynamic Coupe was originally built for display at the 1939 New York World's Fair. Only a few of these cars exist making them among the rarest of French classics.

7. Delage D8 120 Aero Coupé

8. Mercer Raceabout

There are those who consider the Ferrari 250 GTO to be the most beautiful automobile ever created. Its styling is unrivaled by any sports car past or present. Its performance, even thirty-five years after the last 250 GTO was built, still awe-inspiring. The 250 GTO has become the rarest and most desirable road/race car ever to bear the Cavallino Rampante emblem.

9. Ferrari 250 GTO

10. Mercedes-Benz 300SL

One of the rarest and most expensive collector cars known, the Mercedes-Benz 540K Special Roadster and Special Coupe always rank in the top ten cars of all time.

Any list of the greatest cars ever built will have a Packard Twelve. One of the best-built cars of the 1930s, more Packard Twelves exist today than almost any other American classic.

The Type 57S and SC Bugatti rank among the best styled high-performance sports touring cars of the 1930s. This is a Type 57S Stelvio Cabriolet.

Styling alone makes the Talbot-Lago T150 SS by Figoni one of the most desirable classic cars of all time. The sweptback aerodynamic styling was all the rage in the late 1930s. Once again, only a handful of Teardrop Coupes are extant.

The Mercer Raceabout was one of the most advanced automobile designs of the early 1900s. It is the one antique car that most often appears at or near the top of lists describing the greatest cars of all time.

The most recognized sports car in the world, the Mercedes-Benz 300SL Gullwing coupe is acknowledged as one of the most unique automotive designs of the 20th century. An idea that only worked once. The gullwing door design has spelled disaster for every automaker that has since tried to mimic the original.

THE 100 GREATEST CARS

ALPHABETICAL LIST

1. 1938 Alfa Romeo 8C 2900B Sport
2. 1947 Alfa Romeo 6C 2500 Sport
3. 1953 Alfa Romeo BAT 5
4. 1956 Alfa Romeo 1900 SS Zagato "Double Bubble" Coupé
5. 1935 Auburn 851 Boattail Speedster
6. 1937 BMW 328
7. 1958 BMW 507
8. 1929 Bentley 4½ Liter
9. 1931 Bentley 8-Liter Murphy Convertible
10. 1952–55 Bentley R-Type Continental
11. 1937 Bugatti Type 57S Stelvio Cabriolet
12. 1937 Bugatti Type 57SC Atlantic–Electron Coupé
13. 1939 Bugatti Type 57C Saoutchik Roadster
14. 1930 Cadillac V-16 Sport Phaeton
15. 1937 Cadillac V-16 Aero-Dynamic Coupé
16. 1953 Cadillac Eldorado
17. 1959 Cadillac Eldorado Biarritz
18. 1953 Chevrolet Corvette
19. 1957 Chevrolet Bel Air
20. 1957 Chevrolet Corvette
21. 1958 Chevrolet Corvette
22. 1963 Chevrolet Corvette Split-Window Coupé
23. 1931 Chrysler CG Imperial 8 Roadster
24. 1947–49 Chrysler Town & Country
25. 1953 Chrysler Ghia Special
26. 1960 Chrysler 300F
27. 1948 Cisitalia 202 Coupé
28. 1930 Cord L–29 Phaeton and Town Car
29. 1937 Cord 812 SC
30. 1938 Delage D8 120 Aerodynamic Coupé
31. 1938 Delage D8 120 Delta Sport Cabriolet
32. 1939 Delahaye Type 165 V-12 Figoni Cabriolet
33. 1948 Delahaye Type 135 MS Chapron Vedette Cabriolet
34. 1929 Duesenberg Model J Murphy Sport Sedan
35. 1929 Duesenberg Model J Murphy Torpedo Roadster
36. 1931 Duesenberg Model J Figoni Boattail Speedster
37. 1933 Duesenberg Model J Arlington Torpedo Sedan "Twenty Grand"
38. 1934 Duesenberg Model J Murphy Dual Cowl Phaeton
39. 1950 Ferrari 166 MM Touring Barchetta
40. 1960 Ferrari 250 GT Spyder California
41. 1962–64 Ferrari 250 GTO
42. 1967 Ferrari 275 GTS/4 NART Spyder
43. 1968 Ferrari 275 GTB/4
44. 1968 Ferrari Dino 206 GT
45. 1969 Ferrari 365 GTB/4 Daytona Spyder
46. 1911 Ford Model T
47. 1928 Ford Model A
48. 1947 Ford Super Deluxe "Woodie" Wagon
49. 1955–57 Ford Thunderbird
50. 1964 Ford Shelby "Flip-Top" Cobra and 427 Cobra
51. 1964½ Ford Mustang
52. 1966 Ford Shelby Mustang G.T. 350
53. 1968 Ford Shelby Mustang G.T. 500
54. 1922 Hispano-Suiza H6B
55. 1933 Hispano-Suiza J12
56. 1952–53 Hudson Hornet Convertible
57. 1930 Isotta-Fraschini 8A SS Cabriolet
58. 1950 Jaguar XK-120 Roadster
59. 1967 Jaguar XKE Convertible
60. 1923–25 Kissel Speedster
61. 1965 Lamborghini 350 GT
62. 1967 Lamborghini Miura P400
63. 1932 Lincoln KB Dual Cowl Sport Phaeton
64. 1938 Lincoln Judkins V-12
65. 1940–48 Lincoln Continental
66. 1956–57 Lincoln Continental Mk II
67. 1920 Marmon Wasp Speedster
68. 1932 Maybach Zeppelin
69. 1948 MG TC, 1952 MG TD, and 1954 MG TF
70. 1960 MGA Twin Cam
71. 1886 Benz Patent-Motorwagen
72. 1902 Mercedes
73. 1911 Mercedes Labourdette Skiff
74. 1927 Mercedes-Benz Model K
75. 1928 Mercedes-Benz SSK
76. 1937 Mercedes-Benz 540K Special Coupé
77. 1954 Mercedes-Benz 300SL Gullwing
78. 1957–64 Mercedes-Benz 300SL Roadster
79. 1957 Mercedes-Benz 300Sc Cabriolet
80. 1971 Mercedes-Benz 280SE 3.5 Cabriolet
81. 1911 Mercer Raceabout
82. 1953 Oldsmobile Fiesta
83. 1911 Packard 5–48
84. 1916 Packard Twin Six Town Car
85. 1933 Packard Custom Dietrich V Windshield Sport Coupe
86. 1934 Packard Twelve 1107 Coupe Roadster Convertible Sedan
87. 1933 Packard Dietrich Special Sport Sedan "Car of the Dome"
88. 1939–42 Packard Darrin
89. 1942 Packard One-Eighty Clipper
90. 1953–54 Packard Caribbean
91. 1933–34 Pierce-Arrow Silver Arrow
92. 1948 Porsche Gmünd Limousine
93. 1958 Porsche Speedster
94. 1963 Porsche 901/911
95. 1907 Rolls-Royce Silver Ghost
96. 1921 Rolls-Royce Springfield Silver Ghost
97. 1930 Rolls-Royce Phantom II Brewster Town Car
98. 1931 Stutz DV–32 LeBaron Sedan
99. 1939 Talbot-Lago T150 SS Teardrop Coupé
100. 1946 Volkswagen Beetle

Alfa Romeo

8C 2900B Sport

Right off it is important to point out that Alfa Romeo racing cars were driven to outright victory in the Mille Miglia (the world's most challenging road race) 11 times—a total greater than all the other winners combined. This 1,000-mile test for man and machine first ran in 1927, when a pair of co-drivers took 21 hours to cover the 1,000 miles in an O.M.—a Brescia-built vehicle that also filled second and third. Alfa Romeo ran but suffered mechanical failure.

The next year things were different. Alfa came in first and fourth in 1928, first and third in '29, finished in order first through fourth in '30, likewise in '32, '33, and '34!

In 1935, the first Alfa Romeo 8C 2900A, with displacement increased to 2.9 liters by Team Manager Enzo Ferrari, filled the Mille Miglia's first four places. The next year, the Alfa team driving new 8C 2900B short wheelbase models captured the first three positions with a punched out 3165cc car in fourth.

The weather in 1937 was ghastly but 123 cars managed to start in the downpour. Carlo Pinticuda in a thinly disguised Alfa Grand Prix car was flagged off last. This year, there was a substantial French challenge and a 4480cc Delahaye split the Alfas by finishing third.

In 1938, the French brought some 4.5 liter V-12s and 140 cars started, among them a quartet of 2-liter BMW 328s. This event set new records with Alfa Romeo filling the first four places. The winner, Biondetti, covered the ground in just under 12 hours, an elapsed time that would not be improved until 1953. Unfortunately, the event also set a record for killing spectators and the Mille Miglia for 1939 was cancelled.

The following year something called the Gran Premio de Brescia was held on a triangular circuit with BMW first and third, Alfa second and fourth. And then everybody went to war until 1945.

The Mille Miglia resumed in 1947. Biondetti came back with the magic 8C 2900B. The 2905cc Alfa Romeo came in first, followed 16 minutes later by Nuvolari in a 1090cc Cisitalia.

Alfa Romeo continued to produce race cars after the war but times had changed and the Milanese automaker had to change with them. Alfa now had to consider ways to survive in the competitive postwar auto industry, and the emphasis on racing was considerably reduced in deference to developing the company's first mass-produced road car.

But what of the magic 8C 2900s? Beneath their graceful hoods were equally beautiful supercharged 8-cylinder engines with dual overhead camshafts, magneto, dry sump, and finned aluminum everywhere, never mind the remote four-speed gearbox and the bunch-of-bananas headers. It's enough to make a grown man's palms sweat. Surround it with sleek coachwork by two of Italy's greatest designers, Carrozzeria Touring and Stabilimenti Farina, and the concoction is almost euphoric.

The example shown, bodied in 1938, is believed to have been one of the prototypes for that year's Mille Miglia. It was originally sold to the famous Italian champion Giuseppe Farina, who had a new body built by Stabilimenti Farina. The 2.9 was later imported into the United States by Luigi Chinetti in 1947 or 1948, and purchased by then noted sports car collector Tommy Lee. The Farina car was featured in a 1951 issue of *Road & Track*, and over the years this legendary 8C 2900B has passed through the hands of such noted collectors as Peter Satori and Bill Harrah, and is now in a private northern California collection.

Only 30 8C 2900B Alfa Romeos were produced and no two were exactly alike. The deep V in the front bumper is a signature of this aristocratic Stabilimenti Farina sport body, the only known example by the legendary Italian coachbuilder on the 8C 2900B chassis.

Alfa Romeo
6C 2500 Sport

One of the most beautiful cars of the late 1940s, the Alfa Romeo 6C 2500 was among the first Italian sports cars to go into production after World War II. The superbly styled coachwork by Pininfarina earned the 6C 2500 dual honors: it was one of the last cars to be recognized by the Classic Car Club of America and one of the first to be honored by the Milestone Car Society as a postwar collectable. Subtle in its design, most Alfa Romeo 6C 2500s, such as this award-wining example from the Jerry McAlevy Collection, had only minor exterior embellishments. Even the bumpers, as on this 1947 example, were little more than metal strips.

Equipped with a four-wheel fully independent suspension and four-wheel hydraulic brakes, the Alfa Romeo 6C 2500 Sport and Super Sport models were powered by a race-proven 2,443-cc six-cylinder dual-overhead-cam engine with hemispheric combustion chambers. Sport models had a single two-barrel carburetor, 7:1 compression ratio, and developed 90 horsepower, while the higher-performance Super Sport produced 105 horsepower utilizing three horizontal single-barrel carburetors and a compression of 7.5:1.

The car's striking shape was actually narrower at the rear than the front, which led to the unusual three-passenger front bench seat, divided by a smaller driver's cushion, and a cozy two-passenger rear seat. Alfa owners had to be well coordinated since the cars were right-hand drive, with a four-speed shifter mounted on the left side of the steering column!

The 6C 2500 interiors were superbly appointed with jewel-like instruments, faux-yellow ivory control knobs, and luxurious upholstery of glove-soft leather. Such fine detail was a hallmark of these last almost hand-built Alfa Romeo tourers.

1947 ALFA ROMEO 6C 2500 SPORT

Alfa Romeo

BAT 5

While never put into actual production, the Alfa Romeo BATs formed the basis for an entire generation of stunning postwar Alfa models. Designer Franco Scaglione penned three versions of the winged aerodynamic body, this being the first, BAT 5, completed in 1953 by Carrozzeria Bertone. The BAT (Berlinetta Aerodynamica Tecnica) series was created to test aerodynamic designs in the hopes of increasing the performance of postwar models without having to develop newer, more powerful engines. Indeed, the wind-cheating BATs did just that, leading to Alfa Romeo's streamlined designs of the 1950s and such popular models as the 1955 Giulietta Sprint, of which nearly 40,000 were built. The Alfa Romeo BATs are truly among the greatest designs of all time.

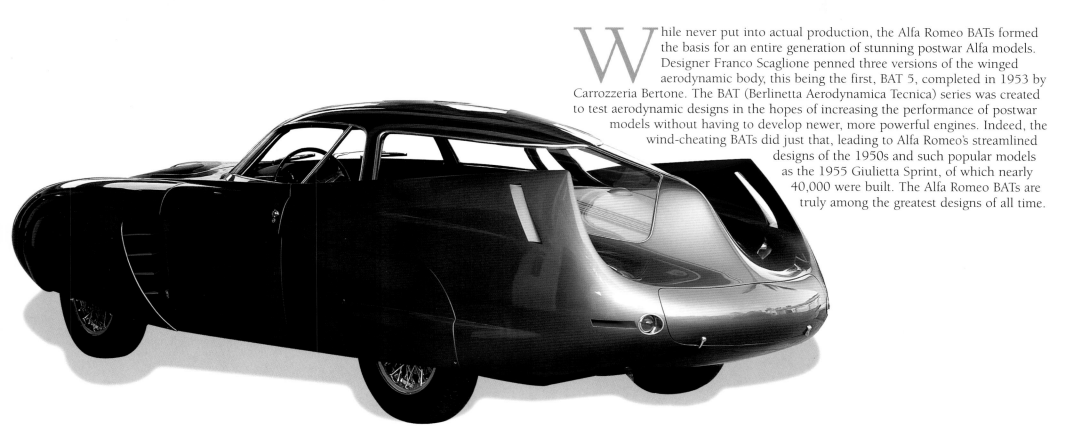

6

1953 ALFA ROMEO BAT 5

Alfa Romeo
1900 SS Zagato "Double Bubble" Coupé

Sports cars of the Fifties were fairly crude. Rough riding, hard to handle, with temperamental engines, carburetors that seemed to go out of adjustment if you looked at them the wrong way, and interiors that were neither luxurious nor comfortable. The Alfa Romeo 1900 SS was guilty of many of these shortcomings, but was nevertheless irresistible as only an Italian sports car can be.

The 1900 was a simple design, devoid of contrivances. One drove it more by sense of feel, sound, and occasionally smell. There were instruments that supplied the numbers, but it was the clatter of the engine, the whine of the transmission, and the feel of the road faithfully delivered through the steering that kept the driver in amiable concert with this car.

Despite a modest price, the Alfa Romeo 1900 was an exceptionally well-built automobile. Inside, there was nothing but steel and leather to surround driver and passengers, but that was enough. The graceful sweep of the dashboard and setting of the instruments was perfect, the leather upholstery flawless. It was as unpretentious interior, done with style and character that needed no embellishment.

Beneath the graceful coachwork was an engine that looked like it belonged in a race car, not in a model intended to be Alfa's least expensive postwar offering. The 1900 was powered by a twin-cam, four-cylinder engine that could propel the Alfa down the autostrada at 100 mph, and do it all day long. Reason enough that the production sedans became popular with *carabinieri* and cabbies, as well as amateur racers throughout Italy.

Prior to the postwar era, Alfa Romeo had never manufactured cars in significant numbers, and after nearly 30 years of offering virtually hand-built sports and racing cars, the idea of mass producing an automobile was revolutionary. However, in the early 1950s, few people in Italy, or anywhere else in Europe, were purchasing

1956 ALFA ROMEO 1900 SS ZAGATO "DOUBLE BUBBLE" COUPÉ

coachbuilt cars. Alfa needed to produce a more affordable model in order to survive. The unibody construction 1900 was the perfect solution.

The first 1900 sedan was shown at the Turin Salon on May 4, 1950. Alfa was quick to stress the racing heritage of the new model, but it was obvious that they would need a Grand Turismo coupé to round out the model line. And Alfa rounded it out quite nicely in the 1950s with a variety of sporty coupés and convertibles on the 1900 platform.

Of the *carrozziere* catering to Alfa Romeo in the postwar era—principally Touring, Pininfarina, Zagato, and Ghia—Zagato was by far the most exotic in its design approach. The Zagatos had somewhat sportier interior appointments, intended for buyers who would use their Alfa as both road and race car.

Of the varied designs, the 1956 Zagato double bubble coupé was the most exquisite, albeit limited to just two examples out of 30 similar cars bodied for Alfa Romeo on the 1900 platform. The 1900 SS Z pictured, owned by David Sydorick, has the standard, and befuddling five-speed synchromesh, steering-column-mounted gearbox, 1975cc 115-horsepower engine, and Lusso (luxury) interior appointments.

The curvaceous Zagato body with its unique low-nose front, elegant curved windows, and flush-mounted door handles was the result of extensive aerodynamic research combined with a certain degree of original styling. The double bubble roof was but one element in the car's extraordinary chameleon-like form. Viewing it from the rear, there were traces of early Aston Martin DB; in profile, Pininfarina for Ferrari's 212 chassis; head on, undeniably Alfa Romeo; from above something altogether different.

Zagato-bodied cars were favored by many of Europe's most prominent racing stables, and Zagato coupés were raced with some success in Italy during the late 1950s. They were also used by several factory works drivers to tour the Mille Miglia course for practice in 1956.

The Milanese coachbuilder had been producing competizione bodies for Italian automakers since the 1920s, having built its reputation with Alfa Romeo creating the coachwork for the great 6C 1500, 1750, and 8C 2300. Today, many of Alfa Romeo's most revered models bear the signature of Ugo Zagato, but only two Alfa Romeo 1900 SS double bubble coupés—one the greatest sports car designs of all time—can claim that honor.

Auburn 851
Boattail Speedster

The American automotive industry emerged for the most part from the carriage trade, wagon makers like the Studebakers who, among other things, built the great Conestoga wagons used to move America west in the late 1800s. The same was true for the Auburn Automobile Company, which evolved from the humble wagon works of two Auburn, Indiana, brothers: Frank and Morris Eckhart.

In 1903 they introduced a chain-driven, single-cylinder runabout, a simple, affordable horseless carriage for turn-of-the-century motoring enthusiasts. Always looking for ways to make a better product, by 1912, they had advanced to building six-cylinder cars of exceptional quality, which they sold at very reasonable prices—perhaps too reasonable. Although their motorcars were popular, the Eckhart's never managed to stay in the black for long; in fact, red should have been their company color. By 1919 they were faced with a choice between certain bankruptcy or selling a controlling interest in their company in order to stay afloat. They opted for a partnership with a consortium of Chicago bankers and businessmen, including chewing gum king William Wrigley, Jr.

With a resuscitated bank account, the Eckharts were able to produce a line of improved models, but even with Wrigley and his monied associates holding the purse strings, the one thing Auburn still lacked was an effective marketing organization. In no time, red ink was once more flowing from Auburn's ledger pages with fewer than 4,000 cars sold between 1919 and 1922. Two years later production slipped to a dismal six units a day, and there were more than 700 unsold touring cars sitting in the company parking lot on the day 30-year-old marketing genius Errett Lobban Cord arrived in Auburn.

Cord was asked to step in and take over as general manager. With his finely tuned marketing skills, some paint, and a few inexpensive modifications to the foundering inventory, he unloaded all of Auburn's left-over cars, netting the company enough cash to pay off its outstanding debts. Cord was promoted to vice president and by 1926 he had ascended to the presidency and become the chief stockholder of the Auburn Automobile Company.

Under his guidance, the company prospered throughout the late 1920s, gained a modest reputation in motorsports, upgraded its dealer network, and had passed an annual sales goal of 20,000 cars by the time the New York Stock Exchange plunged over the edge in October 1929.

In spite of the Depression, Auburn production soared to a record 32,301 units in 1931, the result of Cord's dealer expansion program, plus an all-eight-cylinder line of beautiful, luxurious, and bargain-priced models. Unfortunately, as the 1930s wore on the economy failed to rebound as most had expected, and by 1933 Auburn sales had plunged to a dismal 4,636, and in 1934 only 4,703 cars were delivered.

In a last-ditch effort to reignite Auburn sales, E. L. Cord made a bold—some might call it foolhardy—move in 1934, spending $500,000 to redesign the entire Auburn model line. Duesenberg president Harold T. Ames was put in charge of the company and Duesenberg's chief designer, Gordon Miller Buehrig, and engineer August Duesenberg, were given a free hand to rebuild Auburn. When the new models failed to increase sales, Buehrig was given a modest $50,000 and told to do what he could to upgrade Auburn styling once more for 1935. "With a fifty-thousand-dollar budget, we couldn't do much,"

Gordon remarked years later. "The decision was made to do nothing to the chassis or body and concentrate on the front end sheet metal and fenders." Augie Duesenberg was handed the 1935 engine assignment, in conjunction with Schwitzer-Cummins and Lycoming, which yielded a new supercharged 279.2-cubic-inch eight-cylinder engine developing 150 horsepower. The new 1935 lineup was introduced in June 1934.

Despite what could only be deemed a dazzling selection of cars—cabriolets, broughams, phaetons, sedans, and the 851 Boattail Speedster, such as this luminous yellow model from Otis Chandler's Vintage Museum of Transportation & Wildlife, Auburn sold only 7,000 cars by 1936.

The 851 Boattail Speedster became the most famous Auburn model ever built, a car with all the character and vitality of a Duesenberg, the very ideal Buehrig and Ames had had in mind. It was fast—guaranteed, in fact, to exceed 100 mph, and so stated on a dashboard plaque that read: "This certifies that this Auburn automobile has been driven 100.8 miles per hour before shipment." And it was signed by land-speed record holder Ab Jenkins.

The Auburn 851 was sporty, shaped like a comet, big headed, and wide fendered, with four exhaust pipes cascading out of the left hood side panel. There was just a hint of a cockpit, resembling an airplane's more than an automobile's, with the remainder of the body consumed by a sleek, tapered boattail and pontoon fenders. "The 851 was the most flamboyant American car design of its time," says Dave Holls. A virtual icon for speed, it was everything but Auburn's savior. A total of 500 were built between 1935 and 1936 (the latter as the Auburn 852). Alas, the 1937 Speedsters never arrived. Nor did any other Auburn model.

BMW 328

One of the greatest pre-World War II sports cars ever built came from a company that had never designed or produced an automobile of its own until 1933. That company was BMW.

In the early days of World War I, the needs of the new flying military had far outstripped the manufacturing capabilities of the Austro-Hungarian Empire, and it fell upon the management of Austro-Daimler (an independent offshoot of Daimler Motoren Gesellschaft in Germany) to escalate the production of aero engines. In order to accomplish this, A-D went looking for a subcontractor and found Karl Friedrich Rapp, a Munich engine builder with a small but proficient factory. On March 17, 1916, Rapp put his signature on an agreement with Austro-Daimler to build V-12 aero engines. This arrangement, forged by A-D's agent, a well-connected engineer named Franz Joseph Popp, included the transformation of Rapp Motoren Werke GmbH into Bayerische Motoren Werke GmbH: BMW.

The sudden good fortune of his alliance with Austro-Daimler encouraged Herr Rapp to expand his manufacturing facilities. Unfortunately, whatever engineering skills he possessed were significantly offset by an astounding deficiency in business management. He expanded too rapidly, depleting the cash reserves necessary to operate the plant, and when he could no longer meet payrolls and pay suppliers, Franz Popp brought in a friend, banker Camillo Castiglioni, head of Wiener Bankverein, who willingly increased Rapp's capital in exchange for shares in BMW. Once Castiglioni became the majority stockholder, he gave Herr Rapp the proverbial boot and appointed Franz Popp director.

Under his guidance, BMW's fortunes continued to grow throughout World War I, and the company would have done even better had it not been for the fact that

Germany lost the war. After the war, all of BMW's contracts were canceled, and as a condition of the Versailles Treaty, Germany was forbidden to produce aircraft engines. The Luftwaffe was grounded, and so was BMW.

With time on his hands, BMW's chief engineer, Max Friz, designed a somewhat revolutionary new motorcycle, one that was light-years ahead of anything else on two wheels, and in 1923, BMW introduced its first motorbike at the Paris exhibition. Powered by a flat air-cooled twin-cylinder engine delivering output to the rear wheel via shaft rather than conventional chain drive, it marked the rebirth of BMW. By 1927, nine different models had been created and there were more than 28,000 BMW motorcycles on the road.

The company's prosperity reached an all-time high in 1928 when BMW acquired the Dixi Automobil Werke AG of Eisenach, becoming Germany's second largest manufacturer of small, affordable cars virtually overnight. The little four-cylinder BMWs were actually the German version of the Austin Seven, which had been licensed to the former Dixi Automobil Werke by Sir Herbert Austin.

In less than a decade BMW had become one of Germany's charmed industrial elite, and the company's entry into the automotive market couldn't have been better timed. Barely a year after BMW took over the Eisenach auto plant, the New York Stock Exchange went spiraling into the Wall Street gutter. By the middle of 1930, nearly a decade of prosperity came to a screeching halt on both sides of the Atlantic.

Here, in the midst of economic chaos, was BMW, builder of cheap cars and motorcycles, about the only means of transportation most Germans could afford, if they could afford any at all.

As the European economy started to regain its

1937 BMW 328

strength, BMW took another bold step, introducing its own series of six-cylinder cars, the model 303, in 1933. Having launched itself into the middle-class market, BMW quickly followed up with the model 315 and the sporty 319 in 1934, and with larger displacement engines, the 319/1 in 1935 and the 326 coupé and convertible in 1936, and in 1937, the 327 coupé and cabriolet and the stunning BMW 328 roadster, a car destined for greatness.

Fortune favored the new 328 Sport Roadster from the day of its introduction. BMW management had decided that instead of a traditional public showing for the new model, a works prototype would be entered in the June 14, 1936, Eifelrennen at the Nürburgring. Competing in the class for unsupercharged cars up to 2 liters, the lightweight 328 roadster handily won the event, earning the immediate respect of sports car enthusiasts across Germany.

An evolutionary design, the 328 used BMW's proven rigid tubular chassis, live rear axle, and transverse leaf spring independent front suspension, all inherited from the lively 319 rally car. The 328 became the world's fastest standard-production sports car, capable of zero-to-60 in 10 seconds and a top speed of 95 miles per hour. At its core was an innovative six-cylinder engine with hemispherical combustion chambers. Designer Rudolf Schleicher utilized a novel valve-activating gear that eliminated the need for dual-overhead camshafts, and thus the commensurate chain noise and oiling problems associated with hemi engines of the period.

By 1939, BMW 328s had scored more than 100 victories in European competition, including class wins in the 1937 Tourist Trophy and the International Austrian Alpine Trials. The cars were triumphant in the 1938 French Alpine Rally and the Mille Miglia, at Chimay, Antwerp, a special 2-liter race on the occasion of the 38th German Grand Prix, and in 1939 BMW scored a decisive class victory in the 24 Heures du Mans.

It is no wonder, then, that the BMW 328 rises to the top of every list of great automobiles.

The handsome 1937 example pictured is from the collection of Randy Cowherd.

1937 BMW 328

BMW 507

There are any number of reasons why one car becomes the icon of an era while another, with apparently the same attributes, does not. In the 1950s, it was the Mercedes-Benz 300SL Coupé and Roadster that captured the hearts and wallets of sports car enthusiasts the world over, instead of the equally exciting but little-known BMW 507 Sport Roadster.

As an automaker, BMW was in far worse shape after World War II than Daimler-Benz. Though both had suffered heavy damage from Allied bombing raids, BMW had also lost control of its manufacturing facilities. The Bayerische Motoren Werke found its assembly plants split up between East and West Germany. The main factory in Eisenach was now part of the Russian-controlled Eastern Sector, and the Soviet government consortium Autovelo took over production of BMW cars in the East. In the West, the Allied Control Commission ordered BMW's Munich plant dismantled, and in less than a year all of the tooling, plans, patterns, and hardware had been requisitioned and taken away, leaving BMW with virtually no automotive production capabilities.

During the years from 1945 to 1950, BMW rebuilt itself by manufacturing motorcycles, and in 1951 was finally back on four wheels once more with the introduction of the Model 501. The following year a new 2.6-liter V-8 was introduced, along with an improved 502 series and two new models, a sporty two-door cabriolet and a two-door coupé. What BMW needed more than anything else at this point, however, was an image builder, a sports car to rekindle the history of the great prewar BMW 328 Sport Roadster. Enter Max Hoffman.

It seems that hardly any postwar sports car story can be told that does not in some way involve legendary New York automobile importer Max Hoffman. In the development of the BMW 507, Hoffman played a pivotal role by encouraging the company to press ahead with the project, assuring them of a large and wealthy

American market eager for new and more powerful German sports cars. Of course, he was also telling this to his friend Ferdinand Ferry Porsche, convincing him to build more 356 coupés, cabriolets, and roadsters, while at the same time encouraging Daimler-Benz to produce a road-going version of the 300SL Coupe. With Mercedes-Benz, BMW, and Porsche, Hoffman was almost single-handedly building the foundation for the German car market that exists in this country today.

Through Hoffman's efforts, Count Albrecht Goertz was commissioned as a design consultant to BMW in 1954. A former associate of famed international designer Raymond Loewy, Goertz had moved to the United States in 1938 and worked with Loewy at Studebaker until 1953. From his styling studio in New York City, Goertz completed two design studies for BMW in November 1954, both of which were accepted. The final result would be not one but three cars, the 503 Coupe and Cabriolet and the 507 Sport Roadster.

The chassis for the 507 was designed by BMW's chief engineer, Fritz Fiedler, and fitted with Goertz's dazzling bodywork handcrafted in aluminum. Riding on large 16-inch wheels, the Sport Roadster had an aggressive stance, with the power of the body gathered around the fenders like the arched shoulders of a great cat. The passenger compartment was lean on sheetmetal, narrowed at the waist, and fitted with full-length cutaway doors. From the front, the traditional BMW grille was stretched between the headlights, while across the hood a shallow scoop traced back to a narrow cowl and the base of a generously curved windshield.

Powered by a BMW V-8, the 507 had an impressive 150-horsepower output delivered via a floor-mounted four-speed gearbox. Compared with the new 300SL Roadster, the BMW was more gracefully proportioned, with a beauty not often found in sports cars, and on that alone it should have been a rousing success, but BMW couldn't build them in sufficient numbers to meet Hoffman's demands. He had envisioned selling several hundred 507s a year at a price of $5,000 each, but the aluminum-bodied 507s had to be virtually handmade, and by the time they reached Hoffman's Park Avenue showroom, the retail price was up to $9,000 and production was down to fewer than 100 cars a year. At the same time, the all new 300SL Roadsters were more plentiful and cost just slightly more at $10,970. Sales being dependent on production, Hoffman couldn't sell what BMW couldn't build. Total production for the 507 Sport Roadster was limited to a mere 253 cars produced from 1956 through 1959.

More than 40 years later, the BMW 507 stands as one of the rarest sports cars of the 1950s, and in the light of day, one of the very best ever built.

Bentley 4¹⁄₂ Liter

Among so many memorable automobiles from the 1920s, the massive steel-and fabric-bodied 4¹⁄₂-liter Bentleys must stand in any list of the greatest cars ever built. To Bentley purists, the stalwart line of motorcars produced by W. O. Bentley from 1921 to 1931 (the year the firm was purchased by Rolls-Royce) are the only true Bentleys, cars rich in heritage and unadulterated in temperament.

In 1919, Walter Owen Bentley had set out with little more than an idea when he formed the small company bearing his name. The Bentley organization began without a factory, without a showroom, and with only one experimental model in existence. Wrote historian Ken Purdy, "On this slippery foundation, W. O. Bentley and his associates, a devoted lot indeed, erected a company that lasted for only twelve years and in that short time made itself immortal in the history of the trade."

W. O.'s timing was perhaps not as good as that of his engines. He entered the automotive field in the weak post-World War I economy with one of the most expensive cars on the British market, but it was also one of the best. He was a designer of formidable competence with a keen understanding of the demands competition placed upon an automobile's engine, suspension, and chassis, yet the cars he produced acquitted themselves equally well in London traffic or at Le Mans, where they were triumphant in 1924 and again in 1927, 1928, 1929, and 1930, a record succession of victories that would remain unbroken for over 20 years.

Early Bentley owners were mostly enthusiastic young sportsmen, "the Bentley boys" as they came to be known in racing circles—the biggest group of men ever to find prominence in motor sports merely by driving one marque. Victories from the Tourist Trophy Race to Le Mans helped establish the company as Great Britain's equal to Mercedes. However, unlike the renowned German automaker, which sold more cars because of its racing image, Bentley's success had quite the opposite effect. Many who could afford the cars were afraid to buy them, believing that W. O.'s massive fabric-skinned tourers were dusty, oil-stained, top-down racers that only a professional driver could handle. To Bentley's credit, and ultimate

undoing, they were among the first genuine *gran turismos,* cars that paved the way for future generations of sporting convertibles and sedans. The W. O. Bentleys, unfortunately, were more often the object of distant admiration.

Bentley began with a 3-liter design in 1922 and continued to produce variants of this model through 1931. A short-chassis version appeared in 1924, known as the "speed model," capable of 100-mile-per-hour stretches, with surprising power and acceleration. The larger-displacement 4¹⁄₂-liter models, such as the example pictured, from the collection of William B. Ruger, Sr., arrived in 1927, with a more powerful supercharged version coming along two years later, though against W. O.'s better judgment.

Building a supercharged 4¹⁄₂ was not his idea but that of Bentley's chief financier and three-time Le Mans winner, Woolf "Babe" Barnato. Bentley believed that to supercharge the 4¹⁄₂ would, to use his own words, "pervert its design and corrupt its performance," and his beliefs were later substantiated when the majority of blown Bentleys blew their engines in competition.

As a road car it was a truly impressive automobile, however, and for short stints with the blower engaged, problems were seldom encountered, as owners usually ran out of road or nerve before the Bentley engine could do itself in.

In the *Illustrated History of the Bentley Car,* W. O. commented that the blown models "gave us all a good deal of additional anxiety during our already anxious last months . . . [and] cost us a great deal of goodwill, because the supercharged cars lacked the steady reliability which had, from the beginning, been part of Bentley Motor's religion."

Even in normally aspirated form, the massive Bentley 4¹⁄₂ was an awe-inspiring automobile, and in the end, W. O. had to agree that the attraction of the supercharged version was undeniable. He later wrote, "the magic of the supercharger was not yet dimmed. No one could resist its lure . . . and, of course, they were very fast while they lasted."

The 4¹⁄₂-liter Bentleys, blown or otherwise, have indeed lasted to become one of the marque's most coveted automobiles and the quintessential vintage Bentley.

Bentley 8-Liter
Murphy Convertible

A Bentley bodied in Pasadena, California? A Packard with coachwork executed in London, England? A Duesenberg built in Paris, France? As odd as that may sound, throughout the 1920s and 1930s American- and European-built chassis crossed the Atlantic with clocklike regularity. While Bentleys were most often bodied in Great Britain, this 1931 8-liter chassis was shipped all the way to Pasadena, California, where the Walter M. Murphy Company, best known for building Duesenberg bodies, was commissioned to design and manufacture a convertible coupé. Murphy's chief stylist, Frank Hershey, drew upon his experience designing Duesenberg coachwork to create a stunning two-door convertible coupé for the sporty Bentley chassis.

Of this great car, the late historian, author, and automotive designer Strother MacMinn wrote, "It has a perfectly balanced set of proportions that make this car as exciting as it is. There's no artificial styling. It's all basic proportions and beautifully done."

The Murphy Company built quite a few convertible sedans, and even though this is a convertible coupé, it bears that same stock-in-trade look. At a glance, anyone familiar with classic coachwork would have to agree that this car has all of the celebrated Murphy styling cues—long flowing beaded-edge fenders, lengthy hoodline, and a rakishly windshield—the trademarks of a Frank Hershey design.

Hershey went to work for Murphy in 1928. Although he left for six months to work in Harley Earl's new Art & Colour Section at GM, he returned when Murphy offered to triple his salary, and he remained there until 1932.

According to MacMinn's history of the Murphy Company, the Bentley was originally painted black and was to have featured a new dashboard design Hershey had been working on that placed all of the instruments behind one piece of painted glass rather than using a traditional wood or metal fascia. For some reason it was never done on the Bentley, but appeared later on Hershey's design for the 1932 Peerless V-16 prototype, which by no small coincidence has fenderlines and taillights identical to the Bentley's.

Another feature unique for a Bentley but common for a Murphy design is the use of all-metal construction, which the Pasadena firm instituted in 1930. According to MacMinn, "this is one reason why this car survived, because so little wood was used in its construction."

The most distinguishing feature of the Murphy body, however, is that it does not look British. If not for the grille, it could well be a Duesenberg. As a Bentley, though, it stands head and shoulders above many of its contemporaries as one of most handsome designs ever to grace the 8-liter chassis.

Bentley R-Type Continental

Since 1931, when Rolls-Royce acquired Bentley in one of the greatest automotive coups of the era, the line that had been drawn between Great Britain's foremost luxury marque and the sporty W. O. Bentleys that had won LeMans five times had grown fainter and fainter until, in the late 1940s, it was barely visible. The greatest distinction between the two marques had become the Bentley radiator shell, winged B hood ornament, and a discreet differentiation in handling characteristics and performance. Then, in 1952, the Bentley division of Rolls-Royce, Ltd. did something quite remarkable; they built a singular model that would share nothing of its design with a Rolls-Royce.

The special body, known as the Continental, was designed for Bentley by John P. Blatchley, chief styling engineer for Rolls-Royce, and Ivan Everndeen, and built atop the popular Bentley MK VI chassis. The very first car assembled, the factory prototype known as "Olga," after its British registration number OLG 490, established new standards for Bentley styling and performance, rekindling the spirit of the legendary W. O. cars.

Blatchley and Everndeen designed a graceful envelope body with a sweeping fastback roofline that was reminiscent of the great 1938 Embericos streamlined Bentley, and then complemented it with muscular rear fenders that gave the Continental a dramatic stance, as though poised like a great cat about to pounce upon its

quarry. And pounce it could. In 1952 the Continental was capable of nearly 120 mph, making it the world's fastest production sedan.

To achieve such performance, careful attention had been paid to weight, under 3,800 pounds, and aerodynamic drag, allowing the Bentley's 150-horsepower, 4½-liter, six-cylinder engine to deliver the car from rest to 60 mph in a brief 12.5 seconds, and effortlessly cruise the motorway at 100 mph. Few automobiles offered such high-speed reliability combined with the comfort and refinement of the Bentley R-Type Continental.

With few exceptions, the streamlined aluminum bodies were produced for Bentley by H. J. Mulliner & Co., one of England's most revered coachbuilders. Lightweight alloy was also used for the Continental's bumpers and window frames. The interiors were appointed with sporting bucket-type seats upholstered in hand-sewn Connolly leather, the instrument panel and doors superbly accented in walnut, lacquered and polished to a handsome luster.

All but 43 examples out of the 208 R-Type Continentals built between 1952 and 1955 were right-hand-drive. The majority had manual gearboxes, 28 equipped with floor-mounted gear shifts, another 138 with column-mounted levers, and 42 with GM-licensed Hydra-Matic automatic transmissions.

Olga, the first Continental built, differs from the other

examples by having a one-inch-higher roofline and a divided windshield. The stunning silver saloon with red leather interior was retained by Rolls-Royce until 1960, racking up more than 200,000 test miles, and had been scheduled for dismantling when it was saved at the request of well-known Bentley historian Stanley Sedgewick, who purchased the car and remained its sole owner for the next 25 years. Olga was then purchased by former Aston-Martin and Pace Petroleum chairman Victor Gauntlett, restored for Mr. Gauntlett by P and A Wood in England, and is today part of a private collection in the United States that includes some of the finest and rarest Bentley and Rolls-Royce models in the world.

A benchmark both for its styling and performance in the 1950s, the Bentley R-Type Continental has become the most desirable postwar model ever to bear the legendary flying B mascot.

Bugatti Type 57S
Stelvio Cabriolet

Ettore Bugatti was to the small region of Alsace, France, what Henry Ford was to Dearborn, Michigan. From around 1910 to 1951, nearly 8,000 cars bearing the Bugatti signature were produced at the factory works in Molsheim, and of the 52 different models manufactured over five decades, the Type 57 has become the most famous to bear the Bugatti signature.

A design and engineering masterpiece, the chassis were fitted with stunning body designs created by Ettore's son Jean, who embarked upon the production of the Type 57 series in 1932.

From the time he was 20, the styling studio had been Jean Bugatti's domain, and his designs were the most dazzling to ever grace an automobile's chassis. What he created in the brief period from 1931, when Ettore turned over control of the factory, until 1939, when Jean was killed road-testing a car that had won the Vingt-Quatre Heures du Mans, have become the most celebrated cars of their time.

The Type 57 was Jean's masterpiece, and from its introduction in 1934, to the assembly of the last models early in 1940, a total of 670 Type 57, 57S (short wheelbase), 57C (supercharged), and 57SC versions were manufactured, more than any other model bearing the legendary horseshoe-shaped grille that was Bugatti's symbol of thoroughbred design.

The sleek, custom Stelvio Cabriolet pictured from the collection of Jerry J. Moore was bodied by Gangloff of Colmar in 1937 for the Pernod family, and is one of only three built with this version of the Stelvio body featuring pontoon fenders and a rear decklid design similar to that of the more rare Type 57SC Atalante Coupé.

The exotic Type 57SC Atlantic-Electron Coupé, (pronounced "atlantique"), with its riveted body fins, was Jean Bugatti's stylistic triumph of the 1930s.

1937 BUGATTI TYPE 57S STELVIO CABRIOLET

Bugatti Type 57SC
Atlantic–Electron Coupé

Unveiled at the 1936 London Motor Show, the striking Atlantic body was originally intended to be built entirely of magnesium, or Electron, the then-favored term for the lightweight alloy. Electron, however, proved too difficult to weld, prompting Bugatti to make a radical decision in the design of the car. He elected to rivit the body panels together instead, thus creating the fins that divide the roofline and fenders. In the end, magnesium was totally impractical and the three Atlantic bodies produced were constructed of aluminum.

The Atlantic design, (see overleaf) which inspired other French stylists to experiment with ovoid shapes, was the first to utilize semiellipsoidal windows and doors, which curved up into the roofline in a manner reminiscent of sporting aircraft designed during the late 1930s.

This is the third car produced, owned today by internationally renowned car collector and fashion designer Ralph Lauren. It was originally ordered by English tennis champion R. Pope in 1937, and was his tenth new Bugatti! A tall man, Mr. Pope negotiated with Jean Bugatti to add one inch to the height of the roofline, which makes this example even more rakish than the other two cars. He took delivery in 1938 and had the supercharger added to the Type 57 eight-cylinder engine the following year.

The Atlantic-Electron Coupé is by far the rarest and most coveted nonracing Bugatti ever built, and in the opinion of many collectors, the most desirable sports car of the classic era.

Photos by Martyn Goddard Courtesy of Ralph Lauren

1937 BUGATTI TYPE 57SC ATLANTIC–ELECTRON COUPÉ

Bugatti Type 57C
Saoutchik Roadster

ontinually searching for ways to cheat the wind, French designers developed a practical approach to aerodynamics in the 1930s, and they achieved it without the use of wind tunnels or computer-aided design. It was done by eliminating the square-cut shapes that had dominated automotive styling since the early 1910s, replacing them with rounded edges, integrated fenderlines, angled windshields, lowered rooflines, fastbacks, and fully skirted wheel openings. Among a handful of cars to bear these distinctive traits were sports models manufactured by Bugatti, a marque revered as much in the 1930s for styling and performance as is Ferrari today.

The Bugatti factory at Molsheim, in Alsace, an occasionally disputed border region between France and Germany, was the source of what many collectors consider to be the greatest sporting automobiles of the classic era. Ettore and Jean Bugatti were masters of enigmatic design, combining art and engineering into everything they built—including the Type 57 engine.

Beneath the hood, the engine was as much a work of art as the hand-built coachwork that surrounded it. The labor that went into its construction and that of the engine compartment itself is almost unparalleled, with square engine covers hand scribed in a vaguely geometric pattern, and a meticulously damascened and polished firewall.

Not to diminish romance, however, the artistic approach was actually a means to an end for Bugatti. In Griff Borgeson's book, *Bugatti: The Dynamics of Mythology*, Jean Bugatti's younger brother Roland explains that the use of

1939 BUGATTI TYPE 57C SAOUTCHIK ROADSTER

so-called Cubist-inspired styling was to accommodate the limited skills of the workers recruited from around Molsheim. "They were not wonderful machinists. Making and fitting flat-sided, right-angled castings and giving them a nice finish was well within their competence. Slab-sided construction was the most simple." So much for the Cubist movement.

That aside, the Type 57's suspension was one of the most intriguing designs in automotive history, and it was not simple. The rear was a typical solid axle using quarter-elliptical springs, nothing exceptional; the front, however, used a solid beam axle with open boxed sections on either end, allowing the semielliptical front springs to pass through the shaft rather than be shackled above or below. This has always made it worthwhile for one to stoop down and look at the front axle of a Bugatti.

On the inside, instruments and controls were relatively simple. There was only one version for the world, right-hand drive, take it or leave it. Bugatti seats were uncomplicated lightweight frameworks upholstered in leather and hinged to flip forward, allowing easier entry to the rear on four-passenger models. Wood was the usual medium for the dashboard, with large gauges placed within clear view of the driver. The simplicity of Bugatti interiors was always in stark contrast to the architecture of the coachwork, which led many owners to request exotic upholstery.

The stunning coachwork on this black roadster, from the collection of Dr. Joseph A. Murphy, was created by Jacques Saoutchik, and this is believed to be the only two-passenger Type 57C designed by the celebrated French stylist. The shape is nearly identical to that of coachwork by Joseph Figoni for Delage and Delahaye and is accented with elaborate chrome moldings used to outline the body, the rear decklid in particular, one of the car's most impressive attributes.

The superb chassis and 200-horsepower engine, which speak volumes on their own, in this instance take a backseat to the singular styling of this 1939 Type 57C, truly one of the most exquisite sports cars ever built.

Cadillac
V-16 Sport Phaeton

One of the most popular Cadillac V-16 body styles of the 1930s was the Sport Phaeton, an elegant stretch of open car with dual cockpits and a retractable rear windshield mounted in the front seatback. The Sport Phaeton gave rear-seat passengers more to look at than a seatback. The stylish Cadillac featured a Jaeger chronometer and a speedometer built into an attractive dash fascia in the front seat-back. The Sport Phaeton has become one of the most prized of all 16-cylinder models.

A total of 85 Model 4260 Dual Windshield Sport Phaetons were produced, with a catalog price of $6,500. This example was sold to film star Richard Arlan through Don Lee Cadillac in Los Angeles on June 6, 1930. It was later used in the 1969 film *The Carpetbaggers* in which it was driven by star Alan Ladd, who played Nevada Smith. Now part of a private collection, it remains one of the greatest automotive models and body designs of the twentieth century.

Cadillac
V-16 Aero-Dynamic Coupe

In the 1930s, Cadillac V-16s were fitted with some of the most exquisite coachwork of the classic era. Fleetwood alone offered 54 body styles, ranging from dashing Sport Phaetons to elegant Convertible Victorias and formal Town Cars to the stunning 1934 Aero-Dynamic Coupe. The majority of Cadillac V-16s—about four out of every five built—were closed cars.

In 1933, Cadillac took a bold step forward in automobile design with another Fleetwood-bodied model, the Aero-Dynamic Coupe, first shown as a concept car by General Motors at the Chicago Century of Progress Exposition. Built on a Series 452-C 149-inch-wheelbase chassis, the car featured a swept-back body with pontoon-type fenders and a streamlined fastback roofline—a look that influenced not only American automotive designs well into the 1940s but automotive styling the world over. In 1934, a Mercedes-Benz 500K competition model featured similar lines and went into production a year later as the Autobahn Kourier. Packard also produced three fastback models in 1934, and Cadillac offered production versions of the Aero-Dynamic Coupe to fit V-8, V-12, and V-16 chassis beginning that same year.

Built on a massive 154-inch wheelbase, the longest ever used on a Cadillac production car, the V-16 Aero-Dynamic Coupes sold for $8,100. Fleetwood produced 20 of the ultrastreamlined five-passenger bodies through 1937, eight of which were mounted on the V-16 chassis—three in 1934, four in 1936, and one in 1937.

The car pictured is a 1936 example owned by William B. Ruger, Jr., who says that "after a few minutes behind the wheel, you really forget you're in a car that is sixty-three years old! I like Cadillac V-16s from the late 1930s because they had a kind of sensational styling that was in many ways transitional between the classic era and progress toward a more modern idea. They managed to carry that off fairly well on many of the styles, but no better than on the trend-setting Fleetwood Aero-Dynamic Coupes."

Cadillac Eldorado

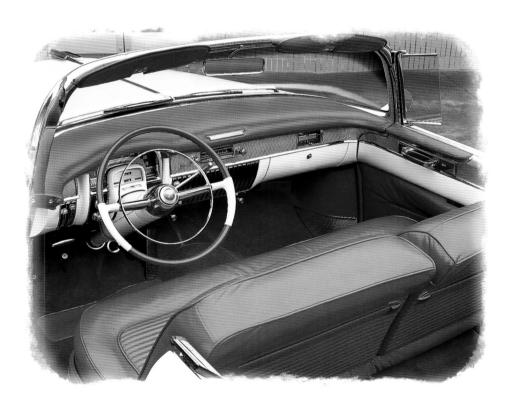

GM's luxury car division created quite a commotion back in 1953 with a single model—the Eldorado. It was the most publicized debut of a new car in history. GM presented the very first Eldorado built to President Dwight David Eisenhower for use in his inaugural parade. A classic press photograph of the 1950s shows Ike standing in the back of the Eldorado, arms outstretched in triumph.

The 1953 Eldorado was a one-year-only model, a special edition limited to 532 examples. More than just a sportier Cadillac, it was a benchmark design, introducing such innovations as the panoramic wraparound windshield, cut-down doors (reprising the rakish look of the classic Darrin Packard), and a flush-fitting metal boot that completely concealed the Orlon acrylic fabric convertible top when it was lowered.

In 1954, the Eldorado became a top-of-the-line version of the Cadillac Series 62 convertible, priced $2,000 lower than in 1953 and built in such numbers as the market would absorb, making the 1953 model one of the most limited-production Cadillacs of the postwar era.

Cadillac Eldorado Biarritz

The Cadillac Eldorado arrived at a time in American history when the automobile was being elevated to the highest status it had ever attained. Americans were car-starved in the early postwar Fifties, and Detroit was rushing headlong into the decade with an endless stream of ideas.

"We in this country created the arsenal of democracy with our plants and manufacturing capabilities during the Second World War. That was a sensational time when we were all tied together, as this country had never been tied together before. And it was out of this atmosphere of pride and accomplishment that we entered the postwar era," explains historian and automotive designer Dave Holls, who joined General Motors in 1952. He retired forty years later as a General Motors vice president and director of design.

Cadillac became Holls' signature car as a GM stylist, and it was Holls who penned the automotive icon of the Fifties, the 1959 Caddy tail fin. "In the early postwar era there was nothing that seemed too wild. People weren't afraid of anything and they were waiting for the most breathtaking thing they could get. It was in this era that the automobile became one of our most important possessions and Detroit became the heart of everything new in this country," says Holls.

It was this enthusiasm that drove GM designers to push the limits of reason throughout the decade, and in 1959 the Cadillac tail fin reached its height, literally and figuratively. The '59 Eldorado was the largest car of the era, measuring nearly 19 feet from chromed bumper to chromed bumper, and the most powerful model Cadillac had ever built, with an enormous 390-cubic-inch V-8 pumping out a gas-swigging 345 horsepower.

1959 CADILLAC ELDORADO BIARRITZ

Completely redesigned as a one-year-only model line, the '59 Cadillacs, led by the Eldorado Biarritz, were the most opulent statements in chrome and fins ever to come from General Motors. Every model had enormous chrome-edged fins soaring skyward from the fenders, with twin bullet-taillight lenses virtually at eye level to most other cars. The '59 fins were so large that drivers often mistook them for another vehicle in their own rearview mirrors!

Rare in the overall scheme of things, only 1,320 of the high-finned, high-powered 1959 Eldorados were produced. Selling for a base price of $7,401, the Eldorado closed out the 1950s as the flashiest American car ever and one that, whether you like or not, still turns heads 40 years later.

Chevrolet Corvette

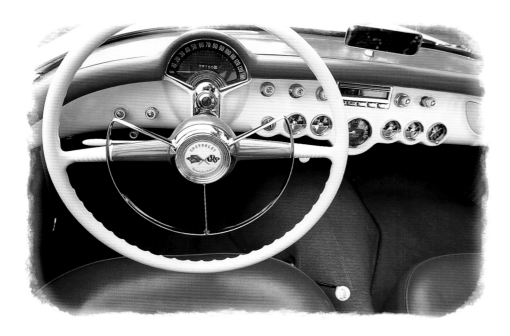

T he 1953 Chevrolet Corvette charted new waters for GM in the realm of automotive styling, captivating a car-hungry American public that was only just beginning to understand European sports car styling in the early post-war years.

The excitement surrounding the Corvette's public debut at the 1953 New York Motorama was due largely to its sleek, futuristic appearance and unique Fiberglas body. Initially, Chevrolet planned to build only 300 Corvettes out of the reinforced plastic material and then switch to traditional steel bodies when the tooling was completed. To GM's surprise, the public was totally intrigued with the idea of a Fiberglas body, and the fledgling plastics industry was so willing to help produce the car that Chevrolet was persuaded to continue production in Fiberglas.

Despite its low-slung European stance and its distinction as the nation's first production sports car, the 1953 Corvette's design quickly drew criticism from consumers. The fact that most people misunderstood the features of the Corvette, or lack of them, such as exterior door handles, roll-up windows, or a serious convertible top, did not reflect an error in design on GM's part—at worst it was malice of forethought. But when it came to the Corvette's lack of performance, Chevrolet was guilty as sin. For the body design, GM's chief stylist, Harley Earl, simply followed the British theory for the construction of a sports roadster. In fact, he based much of the car's design on the Jaguar XK–120. But Chevrolet's engineering department had to answer to a higher authority than Earl. Accounting.

Budget limitations required that Chevy engineers use an existing engine and transmission. Thus the 1953–54 Corvette was powered by a moderately "tweaked" overhead valve six-cylinder engine from the passenger car line, coupled to an automatic transmission, with a mere 150 horsepower and a two-speed torque converter.

Sports car enthusiasts who might have otherwise purchased as many cars as Chevrolet could build were anything but enthusiastic.

Historically, the road to progress is littered fender-deep in ideas that didn't work and cars that after a few short years tumbled from lofty reverence as innovative concepts into the shadows inhabited by motordom's also-rans. This was nearly the Corvette's fate. By late 1954, the car's novelty was wearing thin. The 300 built in 1953 had sold quickly, but now nearly half of those produced for 1954 were languishing on dealer lots. Chevrolet's Motorama dream car was about to become GM's worse nightmare.

The 1953–55 Corvettes were underpowered. Even when the V-8 was added in 1955, the automatic transmission was still inadequate, as were the car's handling and braking capabilities. In 1956, the legendary Zora Arkus-Duntov spearheaded a complete redesign that finally established Corvette as *the* American sports car. But it was the daring 1953 model that started it all, that put Corvette on the road to becoming an American motoring icon of the twentieth century.

The example pictured is an unrestored original and one of the earliest cars produced. It is owned today by well-known Corvette collector Chip Miller of Carlisle Productions in Carlisle, Pennsylvania.

Chevrolet Bel Air

The 1950s, perhaps more than any period since the 1930s, was a decade when automobiles seemed to define the character of the nation, and no automaker did a better job of it than General Motors. Of GM's five divisions, it fell upon Chevrolet to be the standard bearer of the masses—the car most associated with America throughout the early postwar era. In fact, no introduction since the Ford Model A in 1928 signaled a greater shift in the product mentality of U.S. auto consumers than the debut of Chevrolet's 1955 models. Seemingly overnight, Chevy's bold new styling and the availability of a V-8 engine turned the heads of an entire generation that had never before considered buying a Chevrolet. William E. Fish, Chevrolet's general sales manager at the time, remarked that he had never seen a study that said styling was the one thing that made people buy, but he added, "We know it's true."

After Chevrolet introduced its redesigned cars—and image—in 1955, body styles were revised annually, giving each model year a distinctive and easily recognizable look. For 1956, Chevy invested a cool million in tooling to give their front fenders "the Cadillac flat look" and lengthen hoods by four inches. A new grille that spanned the full width of the front end and Buick-style taillights completed a very effective restyling effort. In effect, Chevrolet designs, although essentially unique to the division, were an amalgam of GM styling cues taken from Cadillac, Oldsmobile, and Buick models. The close resemblance to GM's higher-priced lines was the result of extensive deliberation and by no means coincidental. The Chevy Bel Air was often referred to as "the baby Cadillac."

The final phase of Chevy's three-year 1955–57 design cycle culminated with fins and chrome—raising the rear fenders to new heights and accentuating the revised 1957 grillework with Cadillac-inspired bumper guards and a bold Chevrolet bow tie

emblem. The 1957s also gained a sportier stance and a slight reduction in overall height with the use of 14-inch wheels.

It didn't take many words to sum up the source of Chevrolet's newfound popularity. Introducing the 265-CID V-8 in 1955 marked the beginning of a new era, elevating Chevy from the ranks of the relatively unexciting to one of the hottest cars on the American road. By the end of the 1955 model year, there were 1,646,681 proud new Chevrolet owners.

The 1956 models burst on the scene with a grandiose display of performance at Pikes Peak. A preproduction Bel Air driven by Zora Arkus-Duntov shattered a 21-year record by making the 12.42-mile ascent in 17 minutes, 24.05 seconds. (The previous record was 19 minutes, 25.70 seconds.) The road up Pikes Peak climbed through 170 sharp turns and cutbacks to the summit 14,110 feet above sea level and was not only a good test of the car's suspension and handling, but proved the power and acceleration capabilities of the 265 V-8.

"The Hot One's Even Hotter" was the tag line in 1956 advertising, and by year's end it proved to be more than just a sales pitch. Chevrolet closed the books on 1956 ahead of arch rival Ford for the second year in a row and in the number one sales position in the country; 26 percent of all American cars sold in 1956 were Chevrolets.

In an analysis of the American automotive industry, *Fortune* magazine estimated that if Chevrolet split off from General Motors, it would still rank either fifth or sixth in sales volume among all American corporations, ahead of DuPont and Bethlehem Steel and not far behind General Electric.

Chevrolet saved the best for last, rolling out its styling and performance pièce de résistance for 1957. The only way Chevrolet could improve upon the previous year was to come out with an even more powerful V-8—and that's exactly what it did. When the restyled 1957s hit dealer showroom floors, buyers were offered a choice of seven different V-8s with outputs ranging from 162 horsepower all the way up to a whopping 283 horsepower. At the top of the option list was GM's brand-new 283-cubic-inch 283-horsepower fuel-injected V-8 with a 10.5:1 compression ratio. The 1957 fuelie was nothing short of a production line hot rod. With one brake horsepower per cubic inch, Chevy advertising touted, "The Road Isn't Built That Can Make It Breathe Hard!" Coupled with a new optional Turboglide automatic transmission, offering a built-in "kickdown" feature, 1957 fuelies had unrivaled passing power.

As history will attest, the 283 Chevy passed just about every car built in the 1950s, becoming not only the most popular model of its time, but also one of the most prized collector cars ever built.

Chevrolet Corvette

I feel the need. The need for speed!"

Tom Cruise may have made that line famous, but as a species, we humans have felt that need for centuries. The automobile finally allowed us to bring that desire down to a personal level. Even before the turn of the century, gentlemen racers were testing their skills and the mettle of their motorcars in sporting contests. It's in our blood, this need to compete, and in the automotive world it eventually came down to one all-encompassing idea: the sports car.

What Americans recognized as sports cars in the early 1950s were MGs, Porsches, Jaguars, Alfa Romeos, and Ferraris, cars that were unlike anything that had ever been built in the United States. While the 1953 Corvette gave Americans their first taste of Detroit's version, it wasn't until 1957 that the sporty Chevrolet came into its own.

With planning under way for an all-new Corvette to debut in 1956, GM's team of gifted stylists made substantial changes to the original body design. Every aspect was altered and refined.

"All the designers were enamored by the Mercedes-Benz 300SL Gullwing Coupé," recalled Bob Cadaret, who worked as a stylist on the Chevy design staff. "From the windshield forward, the 300SL was the predominant influence on the styling of the 1956 Corvette."

Another principal influence on the 1956 Corvette body came from the LaSalle II roadster, a 1955 GM Motorama car. The LaSalle had coved insets on the front fenders that curved well into the doors and were painted a contrasting color to accent their shape. The Corvette's new fender styling evolved directly from the Motorama car.

With the 1956 models, output from the V-8 was increased to 210 horsepower, with 225 horsepower available through an optional dual four-barrel carburetor. Chief engineer Zora Arkus-Duntov redesigned the suspension, concluding that the 1956 model "goes where it is pointed, and does so without hesitation. On turns taken hard it does

not plow or skid, but gets into the drift. If the right amount of power is fed, the drift can be maintained without danger of the rear end getting presumptuous and assuming the position of the front." With the V-8, standard synchromesh three-speed manual transmission, and revised suspension, the Corvette finally emerged as a true driver's automobile.

The contemporary body style, with convertible or removable hardtop, locking doors, roll-up windows, and more comfortable interior, was designed to meet the needs of those consumers who wanted comfort and convenience. In 1957, the needs of performance were also addressed by Duntov with the introduction of fuel-injection, increasing output to 283 horsepower (one bhp per cubic inch with the top-of-the-line 283-CID V-8), the high-rev Duntov cam, giving optional 2 x 4 carb engines higher performance, a four-speed manual gearbox, and optional positraction rear end. Most of these features were geared toward competition. In the 1950s, race driver John Fitch, who had driven for the Mercedes-Benz team, noted that "The [Corvette's] been the despair of a number of foreign manufacturers— Porsche and Jaguar, to mention two, and it's certainly a contender with the ten thousand dollar and twelve thousand dollar Ferraris." This was music to GM's ears.

The 1958 models were another benchmark in the Corvette's evolution. The revised body design picked up several styling cues from GM design chief Bill Mitchell's 1956 Corvette SR–2 race car, including the air outlets mounted at the rear of the SR–2's coves. On the '58 through '62 production cars, they were reversed and placed at the front of the coves just behind the wheels and were nonfunctional.

Styling changes for 1958 increased overall length of the body from 168 inches to 177.2 and added almost 2 inches to overall width, extending the span from 70.5 inches to 72.8.

The interior of the '58 Corvette was also completely redesigned. The dash panel featured a large dome-shaped 160-mph speedometer flanked by sec- ondary instruments—fuel, temperature, battery, and oil—in four recessed cowlings. Protruding from the lower center of the instrument panel was a soup-can–sized tachometer hovering directly over the top of the steering column. The heater controls, clock, and radio were moved into a new center dash console, making the Corvette one of the first American cars to use this type of design.

The all-new dashboard design featured a recessed cove on the passenger side with the Corvette name spelled out on the curved metal fascia. The interior of the '58 model was so completely new that the only carryovers from '57 were the steering wheel, the shift lever, and the little white pull-knobs that opened the doors. Nearly all of the functional changes in the car were at Duntov's suggestion. By 1958 he either originated, cleared, or approved all of the alterations to the Corvette's engineering and styling.

For the '58 model year, the base 230-horsepower V-8 was the most popular engine, accounting for nearly 50 percent of production. Chevrolet carried over the 283-cubic-inch engine series, offering four versions, two with dual quads, dispensing 245 horsepower and 270 horsepower, and two equipped with fuel-injection. Output for the base fuelie was 250 horsepower. The high-output fuel-injected V-8 was bumped from 1957's 283 horsepower to 290, bettering the previous year's record of 1 bhp per cubic inch. Just over 1,000 of the 290-horsepower versions were ordered, and around 500 of the mild-cam 250-horsepower fuelie engines.

The 1957 and 1958 models pictured are owned by Tom Reddington of Reddington Classics in New Jersey. The '58 is equipped with the 270-horsepower dual quad engine, high-rev Duntov cam, and four-speed gearbox. Reddington's superbly restored '58 'Vette is painted Signet Red with Snowcrest White coves, and his '57 is in a popular Fifties-era shade of Cascade Green (turquoise) with contrasting white coves. The two cars represent one of the finest eras in the Corvette's 46-year history.

Chevrolet Corvette
Split-Window Coupe

I t's interesting how three little words, *split window coupe,* describe the '63 Corvette without any further embellishment. It is one of the few cars in all of automotive history that can be brought to mind without saying the year, or even the make. It can only be a 1963 Corvette.

In one bold stroke Chevrolet departed from the European styling that had guided Corvette design since 1953. The 1963 Corvette Sting Ray rewrote the book, from the four-wheel independent suspension up. The new Bill Mitchell–inspired design featured streamlined styling, concealed headlamps, and for the first time, two distinct models, convertible and coupé.

Engines were completely revamped, from the cooling system to the Rochester fuel-injection system—the first major overhaul of the injection design since its introduction in 1957. The Sting Ray's new engine delivered 360 horsepower and delivered it posthaste, burying the tach through every gear—zero-to-60 in 5.6 seconds, flying through the quarter-mile in 14.2 seconds at 102 miles per hour, and reaching a terminal velocity of 151 miles per hour.

Road & Track, after testing an early production model with the 360 engine and 3.70:1 final drive, wrote, "As a purely sporting car, the new Corvette will know few peers on road or track. It has proved, in its 'stone-age form,' the master of most production line competitors; in its nice, shiny new concept it ought to be nearly unbeatable."

Car and Driver declared the Sting Ray "second to no other production car in road-holding and still the most powerful."

The '63 Corvettes brought many new owners into the Chevy fold, and sales for 1963 came in at an almost even split between the Sting Ray Coupe at 10,594 sales and the new Sting Ray Roadster selling just a handful more at 10,919 cars.

The biggest criticism Chevrolet suffered was over the Sting Ray's split window. In *Corvette: America's Star-Spangled Sports Car,* author Karl Ludvigsen cataloged the litany of editorial barbs:

Road & Track: "Our only complaint about the interior was in the coupe, where all we could see in the rear view mirror was that silly bar splitting the rear window down the middle."

Car Life: "The bar down the center of the rear window makes it all but impossible to see out via the rear view mirror."

Motor Trend: "The rear window on the coupe is designed more for looks than practicality, and any decent view to the rear will have to be through an exterior side-view mirror."

Car and Driver: "Luggage space is surprisingly roomy but central window partition ruins rear view."

And from Europe, *Autocar* remarked: "Nothing can be seen of the tail through the divided rear window, which makes reversing in confined quarters rather precarious."

Criticism aside, the split window was approved

by GM design chief Bill Mitchell, despite the fact that Duntov was against it from the first design drawings to come from stylist Larry Shinoda's drafting table. If the split window was a battle of wills between GM's head of design, Bill Mitchell, and the company's engineering virtuoso, Duntov prevailed. In 1964 the split was gone.

But the 1963 Split-Window Coupe became a one-year-only model that would launch a new generation of Corvettes and become one of the most collectible cars in Chevrolet history, which makes the argument between Mitchell and Duntov a split decision.

55

Chrysler CG
Imperial 8 Roadster

While the average man desiring a sporty, distinctive car may have worked long and hard to purchase a 1931 Ford Deluxe Roadster—Ford sold over 53,000 in 1931 at a starting price of just $475—he would have had to work a lot harder to buy a '31 Chrysler CG Imperial 8 Roadster. Only 100 people did. Priced at $3,220, the CG had its own version of Chrysler's new straight eight, displacing 385 cubic inches and developing 125 horsepower. The LeBaron Chryslers, looking suspiciously like the Cord L–29, used sharply pointed V-type radiator shells, broadly sweeping fenders, sloping split windshields, and extremely long hoods—a combination of features that perfectly defines the look of a classic car today.

The Imperial 8 was a true Roadster, absent of rollup windows and using drop-in side curtains LeBaron's, Ralph Roberts lavished the interior with subtle leather including the door panels, door caps, and dash board. It was as luxurious as a car of such sporty pretention dared be.

1931 CHRYSLER CG IMPERIAL 8 ROADSTER

Chrysler
Town & Country

S oon after World War II came to an end, Detroit automakers found themselves faced with an interesting problem: how to produce new cars from old prewar tooling. One very clever solution used by both Ford and Chrysler was to capitalize on an even older idea, applying wood panels to the exterior of the car's body. Wood panels had been used on station wagons by Detroit automakers (and others) as far back as the 1920s, and wood planking as an exterior design element had been used by coachbuilders in the early 1900s, particularly in France. Faced with the need to distinguish postwar models that had had few, if any, sheetmetal changes since 1942, both Ford and Chrysler decided to produce sedans and convertibles accented with wood.

In 1946, Chrysler introduced the Town & Country convertible built atop the C–39 series 127.5-inch wheelbase chassis and powered by the 135-horsepower flat-head Spitfire eight. In addition there was a companion four-door sedan, mounted on the C–38 series 121.5-inch platform and equipped with the 114-horsepower L-head six. The Town & Country four-door sedan and two-door convertible proved to be relatively popular models. From 1946 to 1948, a total of 3,994 sedans and 8,368 convertibles were produced. One of the most innovative ideas of the postwar era, the Town & Country has earned itself a place among the 100 greatest cars.

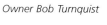

Owner Bob Turnquist

Owner George Cummins

1953

Chrysler
Ghia Special

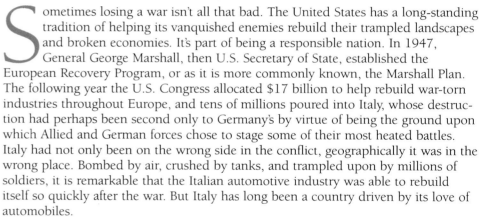

Sometimes losing a war isn't all that bad. The United States has a long-standing tradition of helping its vanquished enemies rebuild their trampled landscapes and broken economies. It's part of being a responsible nation. In 1947, General George Marshall, then U.S. Secretary of State, established the European Recovery Program, or as it is more commonly known, the Marshall Plan. The following year the U.S. Congress allocated $17 billion to help rebuild war-torn industries throughout Europe, and tens of millions poured into Italy, whose destruction had perhaps been second only to Germany's by virtue of being the ground upon which Allied and German forces chose to stage some of their most heated battles. Italy had not only been on the wrong side in the conflict, geographically it was in the wrong place. Bombed by air, crushed by tanks, and trampled upon by millions of soldiers, it is remarkable that the Italian automotive industry was able to rebuild itself so quickly after the war. But Italy has long been a country driven by its love of automobiles.

In the late 1940s, Fiat invited the Chrysler Corporation to Italy to help train Fiat's technicians in the latest American machining and assembly techniques. This same process also helped Alfa Romeo turn into a volume automaker in the early postwar years with aid from the Marshall Plan. In exchange, Chrysler learned a great deal about the Italian automaking industry and the small but thriving *carrozziere,* which were among the last custom coachbuilding firms in the world.

Although Chrysler initially approached Ferrari coachbuilder Pininfarina to build prototype bodies in 1950, a year later it signed an agreement with Carrozzieria Ghia in Turin to build a series of cars based upon designs by renowned stylist Virgil Exner, who had been personally recruited by Chrysler boss K. T. Keller to head up Chrysler's advance design studio.

Exner's first step was to commission a series of concept cars, and by taking advantage of the low cost of construction in postwar Italy, along with Ghia's fine craftsmanship, he was able to produce some of the most beautiful and influential concept cars ever to flow from a designer's pen: the d'Elegance, the DeSoto Adventurer II, the Dodge Firearrow, the Chrysler Falcon, and the Chrysler-Ghia series, all of which helped put Chrysler at the forefront of American automotive styling by the late 1950s.

Among the rarest models produced during the 15-year alliance between Chrysler and Ghia were the Ghia Specials manufactured from 1951 through 1954. The majority were built on the standard 125½-inch-wheelbase chassis used on all Chrysler models (except the Imperial) in 1953. Powered by Chrysler's 331-cubic-inch 180-horsepower hemi V-8, Ghia models were equipped with either the new

Power Flite two-speed automatic or the older Fluid Torque transmission, depending upon when they were built.

The example pictured, from the Houston, Texas, collection of Jerry J. Moore, was delivered in 1953. According to Chrysler archives, this is one of approximately six cars based on Exner's '52 Chrysler Special and '53 Thomas Special. After building the cars for Chrysler, it is estimated that Ghia produced another dozen for themselves.

The relationship that developed between Chrysler and Ghia in the 1950s contributed to the sharing of ideas and designs in both directions across the Atlantic, creating cars that were neither American nor Italian in design and execution, but something new and wonderful. This is something we might take for granted in today's age of international designs, but in the 1950s, the Chrysler Ghias were unique in all the world.

Chrysler 300F

The 1955 Chrysler 300 was the first of the famed letter cars, and the number 300 wasn't just a random choice by some marketing department toady. The 1955 Chrysler delivered a wheel-spinning 300 horsepower when you dropped the hammer. In 1955 that was really something.

The cars were powered by a modified V-8 fitted with two Carter four-barrel carburetors and a solid lifter high-duration camshaft of the same grind American sportsman Briggs Cunningham used in his 1954 Chrysler LeMans engines. The added underhood gear boosted horsepower from the stock 250 to that magic 300 number. For the next decade, these special Chrysler models would be distinguished annually by a different letter in the 300 emblem.

These otherwise nondescript-looking Chryslers began racking up a succession of racing victories in 1956 with a total of 37 AAA and NASCAR titles and an Unlimited Stock Class victory at Daytona, making the 300B the American stock car racing champion.

The first Chrysler letter cars were traditionally styled, truly the banker's hot rod of the era. *Mechanix Illustrated*'s automotive editor, Tom McCahill, aptly described the 300s as "competition cars in a full Brooks Brothers suit." He wasn't far from wrong. The 300s were doing great at Daytona and in motorsports competition, but aside from turning a fast quarter-mile, the stodgy-looking Chryslers couldn't turn heads at a stoplight unless the driver decided to lay rubber for half a block. Then something wonderful happened —1957 and Virgil Exner.

"When I look back at the 1950s I realize that there were some incredible breakthroughs," says DaimlerChrysler executive vice president Tom Gale. "Virgil Exner's contributions during that era were very significant. I think if you go back and talk to guys like Chuck Jordan, who was at GM, they were dramatically affected by what Exner did.

I remember him telling me the story of the time in late 1956 when a few of the GM stylists wanted a peek at the new Chryslers and they went down to the lot to look over the fence and see what was going on. They were just blown away when they saw the '57s on the test track. Exner had a profound affect on everyone in Detroit."

The first and perhaps most dramatic result of Exner's styling influence at Chrysler appeared in 1957, with the totally redesigned 300C. The entire Chrysler model line had sprouted tail fins of exceptional proportions and sleek sporty bodylines that caught GM and Ford stylists off guard. Exner had done away with Chrysler's "old man's car" image in one bold stroke. But he saved the very best for the 300C, distinguished from all other '57 models by a massive grille that virtually consumed the front end of the car. Based on the design of Exner's 1955 Ghia Falcon concept car, the new grille would become a letter car hallmark for years and influence Chrysler styling well into the 1960s. The top-of-the-line 300C carried a 392-cubic-inch V-8 under its hood, packing a whopping 390 horsepower. Leaving its own mark on motorsports history, the 300C continued Chrysler's domination of Daytona Beach by becoming the fastest stock sedan in the world, with a Flying Mile record of 142.911 miles per hour.

For 1958, the letter was D, and the 300s were equipped with the 392 engine, rated at 380 horsepower in standard trim and 390 with an optional electronic fuel-injection system produced by Bendix.

The 300E, equipped with a new 413-cubic-inch V-8 developing 380 horsepower, became a very limited edition for 1959, with only 140 convertibles and 550 hardtop coupes being built.

The end result of Exner's ambition to create the fastest and best-styled automobile in America, the 300F became the greatest high-performance family car ever built. With an optional V-8 displacing 413 cubic inches and equipped with a 30-inch Crossram induction manifold, the 300F delivered an unprecedented 400 horsepower, giving Chrysler unchallenged possession of the American road in 1960.

During the year, 300F models won the first six places in the Flying Mile runs at Daytona, with the winning car averaging better than 144 miles per hour.

The 300F offered a list of options almost as long as the car itself, which measured 18.3 feet from the projecting Chrysler hoodline to the tip of its canted tail fins. Among the most fascinating choices on the option list for 1960 were six-way power seats with dual swivel front buckets, and for truly sports-minded drivers, a limited slip rear differential and manual four-speed synchromesh transmission.

The Chrysler 300F has become the number one letter car of all time and one of the rarest, with only 248 convertibles and 964 coupes produced.

63

1948

Cisitalia

202 Coupé

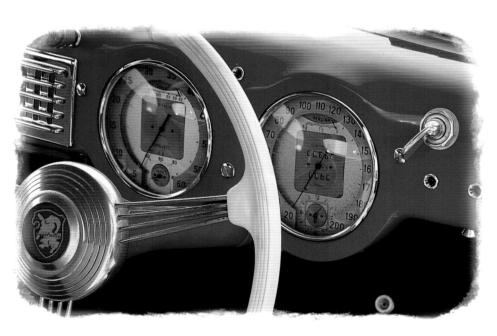

It was World War II and Piero Dusio had managed to be on the winning side—never mind the fate of Italy, his homeland.

When the war ended, he had managed to create a whole class of single-seat race cars, known by the acronym for "Compagnia Industriale Sportiva Italia." Sr. Dusio was running so fast, he couldn't stop before the money just dissolved—one million francs to ransom Dr. Ferdinand Porsche from a French prison, money that the grateful genius would repay by designing the scintillating but unfinished four-wheel-drive, Cisitalia V-12 Grand Prix car. The incidentals for this great leap forward consumed lire at such a rate that Compagnia Industriale Sportiva Italia ceased paying its bills, the magic GP car was shipped off to Argentina, and the music stopped.

But wait—hadn't Piero Dusio also told stylist Giovanni Savonuzzi, "I want a car that is wide like my Buick, low like a GP racer, comfortable like a Rolls-Royce, and light like our single-seater D.46 race car?" He had indeed, and before the lights finally went out, Savonuzzi did a preliminary layout. It was presented to Sergio Pinin Farina, who created the first two Cisitalia 202 Coupes, one pale grey, the other metallic aquamarine.

When the 202 appeared at the Villa d'Este Concours d'Elegance this lovely creation rocked the automobile world with its serene solutions to postwar design problems that hadn't even been confronted yet, and now would never arise.

The Cisitalia 202, such as this beautiful 1948 model from the Caballerzia, Inc., collection, became the first modern sports car, establishing a school of design that would dictate the shape of berlinetta body styling for more than a decade.

A Cisitalia 202 was featured in the 1951 New York Museum of Modern Art (MOMA) show titled "8 Automobiles." In 1972 Carrozzeria Pininfarina donated a 202 to MOMA's permanent collection, where the legendary Cisitalia now serves as an example of machine art.

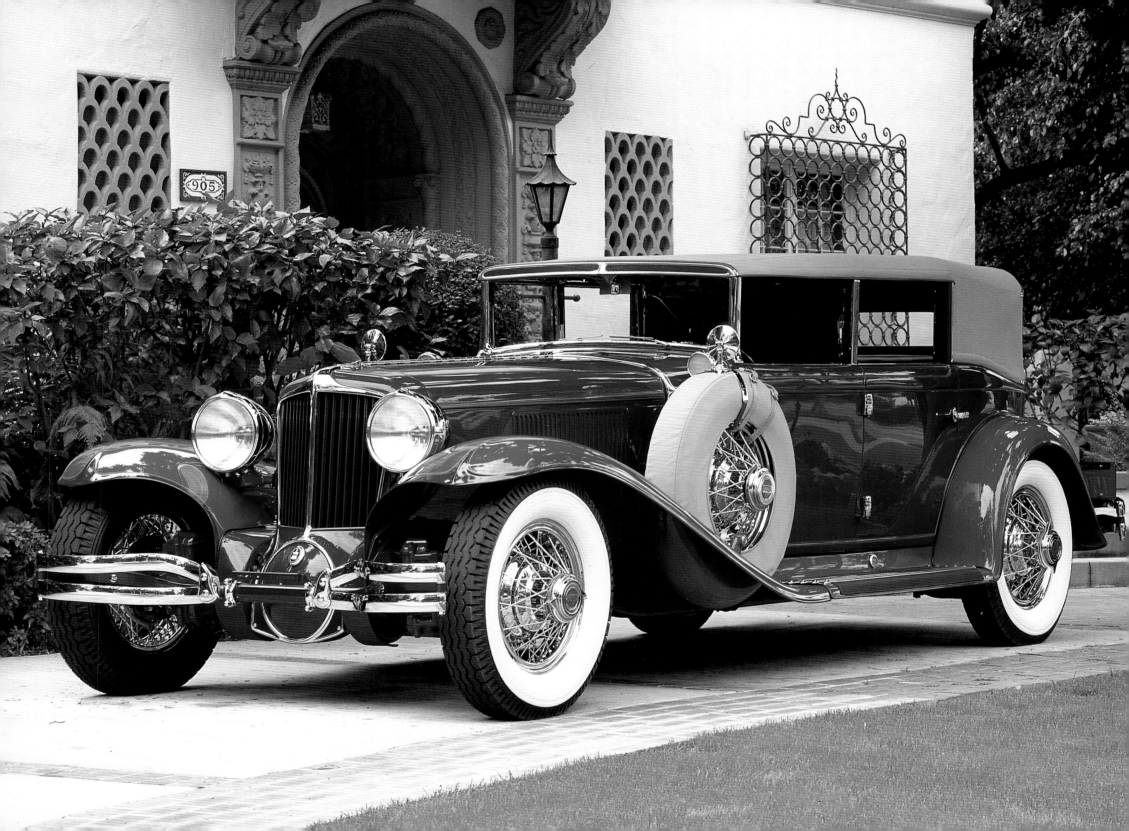

Cord L–29

Phaeton and Town Car

In 1999, we celebrated the 70th anniversary of a monument to innovation, the most successful engineering idea in automotive history, *front wheel drive*. The company that brought this imaginative concept to market back in 1929 was Cord.

E. L. Cord's concept for a car that was powered by the front wheels, rather than the rear, was still considered state-of-the-art 37 years later, when General Motors introduced the front-wheel-drive Oldsmobile Tornado in 1966. As a result of the Tornado, front wheel drive was to become the most touted advance in the automotive industry since disc brakes. In the 1960s, hardly anyone remembered the Cord. Most Americans thought GM invented front wheel drive.

From a certain point of view, General Motors breathed new life into the idea, improved upon its design, and within a decade had made the concept an industry standard. It was a bit more adventurous back in 1929 when Cord introduced the L–29, because front wheel drive had never before been successfully tried on a production car.

Built by a new division of Errett Lobban Cord's flowering Indiana-based automotive and aviation empire, which included Auburn and Duesenberg, the L–29 was a relatively affordable car for the time, priced in 1930 at just $3,295 for a convertible. The L–29 was a groundbreaking design that stunned the automotive world when it appeared in the summer of 1929 as a 1930 model. With international debuts in both Paris and London, the Cord was regarded by the foreign motor press as the first American automobile to capture the spirit of European design.

The crowning achievement of the car's debut year was its selection as Official Pace Setter for the 1930 Indianapolis 500, which, as luck would have it, was won by a front-wheel-drive Miller, the very car upon which the Cord's engineering was based!

The front-wheel-drive system, developed for Cord by automotive engineer C. W. Van Ranst, who had also worked with Miller, was based on a simple premise: turn

everything around. The driveline was laid out in
reverse, with the differential and drive axle in front,
followed by the transmission, clutch, and engine. The
benefits of the Van Ranst design were twofold: better
traction, since the drive and steering wheels were one
and the same, and a lower body height, with the traditional front-to-rear driveshaft and transmission tunnel
having been eliminated. In an era when every change in
automotive styling or engineering was newsworthy, the
Cord L–29 was the stuff headlines are made of.

Despite its technological advances and voguish
good looks, the L–29 arrived at a abysmal time in
American history. The economic tidal wave that had
swept prosperity from Wall Street and most of the
country late in 1929 had greatly weakened automotive
sales, and even with an affordable price compared with
any other car in its class, there weren't enough buyers to
make the L–29 a lasting success. This was compounded
by servicing problems on the front-wheel-drive system
and a general shift away from glitzy cars as the
Depression-torn economy stumbled along. By 1932 the
L–29 was out of production, and it would be 1936
before the all-new Cord 810 appeared. The L–29, however, had earned its place in history as the first production front-wheel-drive American car.

The L–29 Phaeton is from the collection of Len
Urlik. The striking 1930 town car from the Nethercutt
collection was originally built for actress Lola Montez
by the Walter Murphy company in Pasadena California.

Cord 812 SC

The 1936 Cord 810 and 1937 Cord 812 have been hailed as the most beautiful automobiles ever designed, and while there may be dissenting opinions, there is no question that they shocked the automotive industry out of its Depression-born complacency. In one bold stroke of the stylist's pen, Duesenberg body designer Gordon Buehrig brought a dramatic end to the way automotive stylists looked at the front of an automobile. The grille was gone, and so too were fender-mounted headlights. Buehrig had not only broken the traditional rules of design, he had rewritten them.

Gordon Miller Buehrig joined E. L. Cord's automotive empire in June 1929 and was only 25 years old when he was appointed chief body designer for Duesenberg. From his drafting table came some of the most celebrated automotive designs of the classic era.

In 1934 he was asked to design a companion model to the J Duesenberg, a smaller, less expensive car but with equally striking proportions. That proposal would later become the basis for the all-new front-wheel-drive Cord 810. The design was reworked by Buehrig to accommodate the improved front drive platform pioneered with the L–29, but the project was shelved for six months while Cord made the final decision on whether or not to produce the car. The green light came a mere four months before the 810's debut at the 1935 New York Auto Show.

Working in around-the-clock shifts, the company managed to produce the 100 production cars decreed necessary in order to display a new model at the Auto Show. They were completed at the eleventh hour, except that none of the cars were running! Based solely on Buehrig's styling, the Cord 810 was the hit of the New York show. Fortunately no one asked for a test drive!

After New York, Cord set about the task of completing the cars and getting them into the hands of anxiously waiting owners, but it was six months before deliveries could begin.

1937 Cord 812 Phaeton from the Jerry J. Moore Collection

For those who were willing to be patient, what awaited them was the most advanced automobile of 1936. The 810 was literally years ahead of anything else on the road. The Sportsman convertible, such as this supercharged 1937 example from the Dr. Joseph A. Murphy Collection, featured a completely disappearing top and was the premiere model of the Cord line, complemented by a Phaeton and two Sedan models.

Completely different from any other car of its time, the 810 was the first American automobile to have hidden door-hinges, the first to introduce a one-piece rear-hinged hood and concealed headlights, and the very first water-cooled automobile ever to abandon the use of a traditional front grille and radiator shell. Buehrig had indeed broken all the rules.

Beneath the aerodynamic coachwork was an equally advanced driveline and chassis, developed by Buehrig's counterpart in engineering, Herbert C. Snow, the man who pioneered the X-braced frame in American automobiles.

The new 810 design placed the specially built 125-horsepower Lycoming eight-cylinder engine immediately aft of the front axle, with the differential (covered by Buehrig's stylish bodywork forward of the nose and accented by the Cord crest) attached directly to the clutch housing. The new arrangement, coupled to a Bendix preselector vacuum shift transmission, gave the car a near perfect 55:45 front-to-rear weight ratio. The Bendix also did away with the conventional floor-mounted shifter. To select gears, the driver simply moved a small ring through a miniature gated gearbox mounted on the right-hand side of the steering column and then released the clutch.

The 810 and 812 (the latter introduced in 1937 with an optional supercharged engine and Duesenberg-style external side pipes) were exceptionally well-balanced cars, with a lower center of gravity than most and a lower unsprung weight. The powerful Lycoming engine, either normally aspirated or supercharged, delivered quick response, zero-to-60 in 20 seconds, and with the blower, a mere 14 seconds elapsed before reaching the mile-a-minute mark. Equipped with Lockheed hydraulic brakes to bring the high-performance Cords down from speed with ease and reliability, basically everything on the 810 and 812 was done right. It was just done too late to save the company.

In his memoirs, Gordon Buehrig summed up the last days of Cord. "In recording the history of any product or event, it is possible to see how one slight change in circumstances might have altered the results completely. In the Cord, it was the six months of inactivity, when the whole program, then half completed, was stopped. If it hadn't been for this delay, they would have had production cars ready for delivery at show time. They would have had time to correct the little mechanical deficiencies, and their first cars would have been good ones. It is very possible the whole venture would have been a complete and lasting success."

In many respects the Cord was a success, but on too small a scale to keep the company alive. On August 4, 1937, E. L. Cord decided to get out of the automobile business, and the doors at Auburn, Cord, and Duesenberg were closed, ending one of the greatest chapters in American automotive history.

Delage D8 120
Aerodynamic Coupé

In the 1930s, exotic cars bore names like Isotta-Fraschini, Hispano-Suiza, Delahaye, and Talbot-Lago. There was no such thing as a Ferrari or a Lamborghini. In 1939, Enzo Ferrari had just resigned from his position as director of racing for Alfa Romeo to go into business for himself building race cars, and Ferrucio Lamborghini, still working on his family's farm in Ferrara, north of Bologna, wouldn't cross Ferrari's path for another 25 years. In America, few people had heard of cars like Hispano-Suiza or Delahaye, and the better-known foreign marques of the period, Jaguar, Mercedes-Benz, and Rolls-Royce, were the exclusive purview of America's café society. The one foreign marque that millions of Americans did come to know in the late 1930s was Delage. The credit for this feat goes to a stunning trio of cars sent by the French government for display at the 1939 New York World's Fair, where they were seen by countless scores of Americans who had never before had the opportunity to regard a coachbuilt French car.

Of the three Delages commissioned by the French government, the first two were bodied in 1938 by the renowned firm of Letourneur et Marchand for display in the French Pavilion throughout 1939. The third Delage, designed and built by Henri Chapron, Delahaye's premier coachbuilder, was added in 1940, after the fair was extended an additional year by New York Mayor Fiorello La Guardia. All three cars were built on the new Delage D8 120 chassis and powered by a Delahaye-built 4.7-liter straight eight, with a bore x stroke of $3^{1/8}$ x $4^{3/16}$ inches and swept volume of 262 cubic inches. The overhead valve Delahaye eight, like the 4-liter Delage engine before it, was capable of making 120 horsepower at 4,000 rpm, sufficient to run an average car up to 90 miles per hour, and with lighter-weight coachwork, over 100 miles per hour.

The beginning of World War II prevented the World's Fair cars from returning to France, and all three were sold to American buyers for an estimated price of $7,500 each. They have remained in this country ever since.

Delage D8 120
Delta Sport Cabriolet

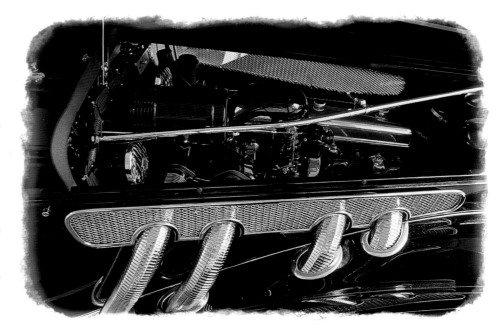

While all three were custom-bodied examples, their styling was indicative of the advances being made in coachwork design by France's leading stylists. The sleek Delage Aerodynamic Coupé featured a *Vutotal* pillarless window pioneered by legendary French stylist Jean-Henri Labourdette. As applied by Letourneur et Marchand, the side windows swept downward following the curve of the body and roofline but had no "B" pillar or other visible means of support. The second car, known as the Delta Sport Cabriolet, had styling similar to designs by Chapron, with a tapered decklid blending into the sweeping rear fenderlines.

The interior of the Delta Sport was lavishly upholstered in red leather. This model also featured the Cotal preselector gearbox mounted on the steering column.

Following another trend established by Labourdette, Letourneur et Marchand used the *surbaissée* construction technique on both cars, positioning the body over the chassis rather than on top of it, thus allowing lower, more aerodynamic exterior styling, with the interior of the car actually lowered between the chassis rails. Both examples also bore stylish external flex-pipe exhausts boldly exiting the hood side panel and cut through the right-front fender.

Throughout the 1930s, French coachwork remained on the cutting edge of automotive design, with stylists working at a level that still bewilders auto enthusiasts more than half a century later. One can only accept that their interpretations of the automobile body were as much an art form as they were a practical means of surrounding the steelwork structures beneath. They created rolling works of art that have withstood the test of time, immortalizing automobiles that have not been built in over half a century.

1938 DELAGE D8 120 DELTA SPORT CABRIOLET

Delahaye
Type 165 V-12 Figoni Cabriolet

One of France's oldest automakers, Delahaye was established 105 years ago in 1894, and along with Peugeot and Renault, pioneered the French automotive industry that prospered throughout the 1920s and 1930s.

By the time of the Great Depression, Delahaye had become known as a builder of "sturdy, reasonable cars for sturdy, reasonable Frenchmen," and it wasn't until 1930 that Charles Weiffenbach, chairman of Delahaye from 1906 to 1954, determined that production of more luxurious coachbuilt models and competition cars would be advantageous. Given an economy divided between the very rich and the very poor, Weiffenbach decided to cater to Europe's café society and leave mass production to automakers like Renault and Peugeot, who were better suited to the task.

A small company compared to many of its European contemporaries, Delahaye set out in 1933 to make a name for itself in racing, no small task given the competition from Ettore Bugatti, Louis Delage, Alfa Romeo, and Europe's mightiest automaker, Daimler-Benz. Delahaye nevertheless cast its fate to the wind and at the 1933 Paris Auto Salon unveiled a new model, the Superluxe with a 120-horsepower 3.2-liter six-cylinder engine, front independent suspension, and large self-adjusting brakes. By design, it was a chassis that could be bodied for touring, or fitted with lighter-weight coachwork suited to sports car competition.

A year later the Superluxe emerged as the Delahaye Type 135, equipped with a slightly larger 3.5-liter engine and an array of coachwork that made the car suitable for everything from cruising along the Champs Elysées to screeching down the Mulsanne straight at LeMans. Fitted with extravagant coachwork designed by Joseph

Figoni, Jacques Saoutchik, and Henri Chapron, the Delahaye would rise to prominence and become one of the most desirable and luxurious automobiles in Europe; the car of kings, emperors, millionaires, and mistresses.

In competition, Delahayes finished an impressive number of races during their brief five-season career, including a first in the '34 Monte Carlo Rally and the Coupé des Alps; a third overall at LeMans in '35, making it the first French car to finish; a sweeping second, fourth, fifth, and seventh in the '36 Automobile Club of France Grand Prix, and a grand victory at LeMans in 1938.

For 1939, Weiffenbach decided that Delahaye needed to do something even more spectacular, and that something was a V-12 engine on the 165 chassis fitted with a one-off body by the master of aerodynamics, Joseph Figoni. The styling was similar to Type 135 bodies, but given the proportions of the massive Cabriolet, the 165 appeared larger than life, literally and figuratively. Only one example was completed, and a second, nonrunning display car was shown at the Paris Salon.

Bodied as a two-seater, which was the competition formula (most Delahayes were designed to seat four or five), the Figoni Cabriolet was one of the French designer's more sedate, yet still seductive, aerodynamic motifs. As with nearly all Delahayes designed by Figoni, the bodywork characterized the image of captured motion—just a trace of windshield frame, which could be cranked down completely into the cowl if one desired, chromed sweeplines slashing through the hood and doors, and bold, elliptical fenders that gave the body a sense of fluidity, as though being stretched rearward by the force of its speed.

Inside, the right-hand-drive Cabriolet was simply appointed with instruments

spread across the dashboard, a large steering wheel, and the optional Cotal pre-selector transmission mounted to the left side of the steering column. The seats and interior panels were upholstered in exotic white ostrich hide with red leather piping, an elegant accent in the best Figoni tradition. The V-12 left most everyone at the 1939 Paris salon speechless. It is much the same today whenever the car appears in public.

Monsieur Charles, as Weiffenbach was known around the Delahaye works, had accomplished nearly all of his goals for the company by 1939, and could have gone even further with the new V-12 had not the shadow of war been cast across Europe. By 1945, it seemed impossible for a small, privately held automaker like Delahaye to pick up the pieces and start again, yet Weiffenbach did just that and throughout the last years of the 1940s Delahaye produced a stunning line of prewar-based chassis and engines fitted with the best coachwork that Joseph Figoni and his contemporary, Henri Chapron, ever designed. Alas, it was not enough to keep Delahaye and Delage, which had been acquired in 1935, in the black.

The market for such cars was small, too small, and Weiffenbach barely managed to keep the doors open. By 1951 production had declined to just 77 cars and three years later the company was taken over by Hotchkiss. In 1956 Hotchkiss built the very last vehicle to wear the Delahaye badge. It was a truck.

Delahaye
Type 135 MS Chapron Vedette Cabriolet

Behold the classic French automobile. More than mere *voiture*. As surely as if brush had been put to canvas or a symphony of notes penned on paper, these wondrous cars of the 1930s and 1940s were a tableau vivant sculptured in steel and set into motion by the hands of artisans.

The hands of Henri Chapron worked harder and longer, perhaps, than any others trained in the coachbuilder's art. The house of Chapron at 114 rue Aristide Briand produced more than 8,000 coachbuilt bodies between 1919 and 1985.

By the early 1920s, Henri Chapron (who died in 1978 at the age of 92) had earned a reputation for creating luxurious coachwork for DeDion-Bouton, Hispano-Suiza, Talbot, Delage, and Delahaye chassis. At one time the Chapron atelier employed more than 250 craftsmen, turning out up to three cars per day.

Like many great designers of the era, Chapron did not sketch out his own ideas, but rather dictated them to an artist, revising the work again and again until it appeared on paper as it did in his mind's eye. Full-size drawings would then be created, followed by wooden styling bucks upon which sheet steel or aluminum could be hand-shaped into finished body panels.

Of all the great French automakers Chapron designed for, his most celebrated coachwork appeared on Delage and Delahaye chassis produced from the 1920s to the late 1940s, and this breathtaking 1948 Delahaye 135 MS Vedette from the Jim Hull Collection is possibly *carrossier* Chapron's finest creation.

The original design for the Delahaye was first shown in 1947, winning that year's Concours d'Elegance in Paris. The name Vedette itself, like many others chosen by Chapron, had no special automotive meaning, as do terms like *cabriolet, phaeton,* or *roadster.* It translates roughly as "movie star."

On the 1948 version, the dashboard was of particular interest, containing an array of controls behind a steering wheel of clear Lucite. The light switch, windscreen wiper control, even the small shift knob on the Cotal electromagnetic preselector gearbox, located on the left side of the steering column, were Lucite. The starter switch, concealed beneath the dashboard, was about the only control that did not have a clear plastic cube or sphere attached to it.

The elegant interior appointments were complemented by a dash panel of hand-rubbed burled wood, with a polished chrome fascia surrounding the controls and radio. The upholstery, as with all Chapron designs, was exquisitely tailored, from the pleated leather seat cushions to the door panels and storage pockets. Even the boot cover was custom fit.

This elegant cabriolet was actually built on a chassis frequently used for racing, a direct descendant of the Delahaye competition chassis and driveline that won at LeMans a decade before.

The 1948 135 MS was powered by a 3.5-liter overhead-valve in-line six-cylinder engine with three side-draft Solex carburetors, producing a staunch 160 horsepower. A quick and agile car with an independent front suspension supported by a single transverse leaf spring, fabricated top links, long radius arms, and a live rear axle pinioned by semielliptical springs, the sporting 135 MS chassis, with proper refinements, could become a marvel of luxury and exhilarating performance combined within a single automobile.

Chapron's design for the Vedette was a true masterpiece, combining the last gasp of classic lineage with contemporary 1940s styling, a body that flowed from front to rear as though extruded from a single block of steel. The pontoon-style fenders and swept-back contours of the decklid gave the Delahaye a profile so bold it appeared to be lunging forward even at rest. It was the last, best example of an era in automotive history that would come to an end by 1950.

1948 Delahaye Type 135 MS Chapron Vedette Cabriolet

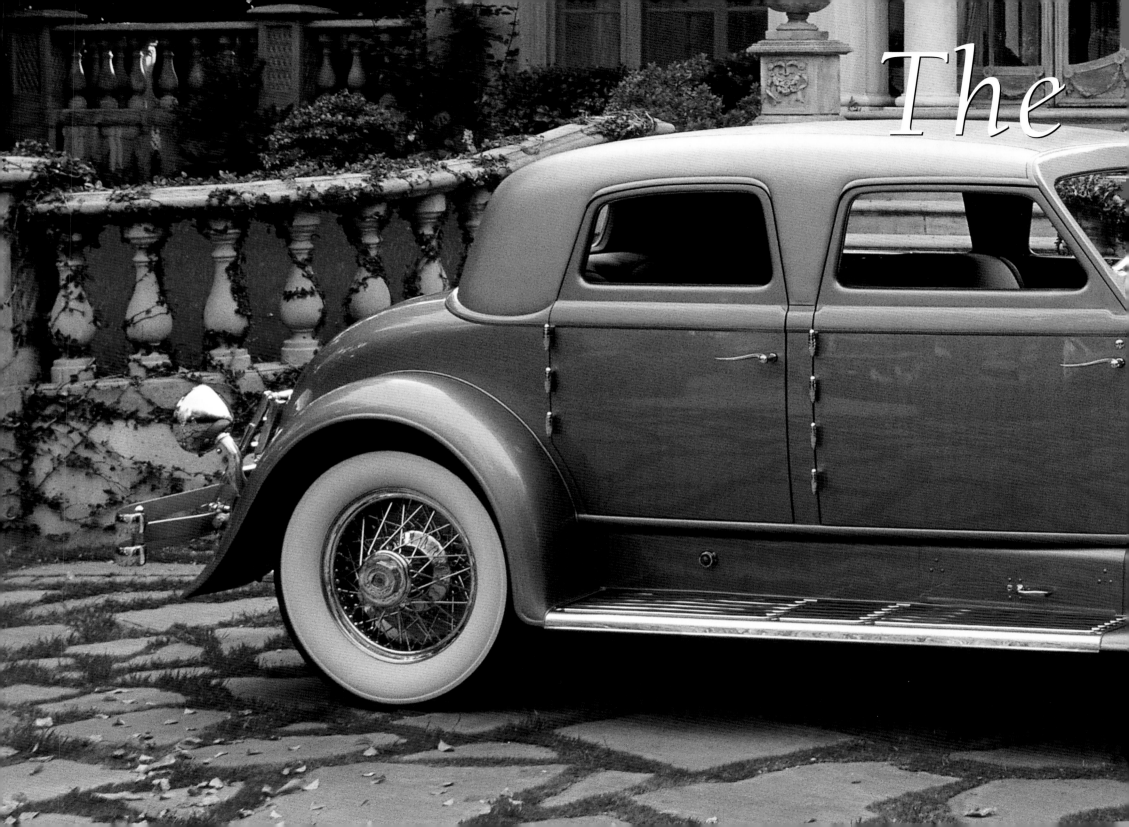

The

Mighty Duesenbergs

Duesenberg
Model J Murphy Sport Sedan

Among affluent Americans, ownership of a Duesenberg took its place alongside lavish estate homes and private yachts as a symbol of success. By the early 1930s, the Duesenberg had set standards no other automobile in America could approach, and in Europe the Model J was regarded with the same esteem as the Mercedes-Benz 500K, Hispano-Suiza J12, and Rolls-Royce Phantom II.

At the heart of the Model J was the remarkably powerful Duesenberg straight eight engine, developing 265 horsepower, and in the supercharged SJ version, an unparalleled 320 horsepower. Both figures were perhaps slightly inflated by the Duesenberg factory, but even so they were head and shoulders above every other car of the era by nearly 100 horsepower.

The big-bright-green engines were revered not only for their performance but for their engineering, which incorporated Fred Duesenberg's race-proven dual-overhead cam four-valve-per-cylinder design. More than 70 years later, dual-overhead cams and multivalve cylinders are still used in high-performance cars.

To manage such power, the Model J chassis was exceptionally strong, endowing the cars with unmatched durability, and every one of the approximately 485 Duesenbergs built between 1928 and 1937, when the last one left the Indianapolis, Indiana, factory, was fitted with a handmade coachbuilt body of extraordinary quality and cost. The price of a Model J averaged from $15,000 to $20,000 during the years of the Great Depression, making it the most expensive American automobile of its time. The chassis alone, without the coachwork, had a base price of $8,500, which was increased to $9,500 in 1932.

Fitted with the most beautiful coachwork of the era, approximately 175 different body styles were designed for the Duesenberg chassis by the leading automotive stylists on two continents.

1929 DUESENBERG MODEL J MURPHY SPORT SEDAN

Duesenberg
Model J Murphy Torpedo Roadster

From the very beginning there were certain features that would become established trademarks, regardless of the coachbuilder. Every Model J came with the distinctive Duesenberg grille, headlights, hood panels, and fenders. With very few exceptions, these design elements, along with Duesenberg's famous engine-turned metal dashboard, aviation-style instruments, and distinctive steering wheel, bumpers, and wheels, were present on every car.

When the supercharged SJ engine was introduced, the original hood design changed to accommodate four impressively large corrugated exhaust pipes, which plunged from the hood side-panels, through the fenders, and beneath the body on the passenger side. Their appearance was so spectacular that many nonsupercharged cars were retrofitted with the pipes in the 1930s, and in recent years most have been so equipped during restoration.

Despite the variety of body designs penned for the Duesenberg, there were basically 10 traditional styles: phaetons, phaetons with roll-up glass windows (also known as torpedo phaetons), convertible sedans (four-door body styles), convertible coupés (two-door body styles), convertible victorias, speedsters, sport sedans, town cars, coupés, and sedans.

The Walter M. Murphy Company, which was located in Pasadena, California, holds the distinction of having produced more Duesenberg bodies than any other builder, a total of 135 in 14 different styles, including the popular Murphy Dual Cowl Phaeton, such as the two-tone green car pictured from the Nethercutt Collection. East coast coachbuilder Rollston of New York built 56 Duesenberg bodies in 11 different styles. Willoughby Company of

1929 DUESENBERG MODEL J MURPHY TORPEDO ROADSTER

Duesenberg
Model J Figoni Boattail Speedster

Utica, New York, furnished approximately 50 in four styles. Derham Body Company in Rosemont, Pennsylvania, built 37 in nine variations. LeBaron, Inc. designed and built 31 in five styles, mostly Dual Cowl Phaetons. J. B. Judkins Company of Merrimac, Massachusetts, produced 21 cars with seven choices in body styling. La Grand, which was Duesenberg's own coachbuilding firm (also Walker La Grand), accounted for 17 chassis in four styles, plus two custom-built short-wheelbase Speedsters—one built for Gary Cooper and another for Clark Gable. The Weymann American Body Company, specializing in the patented Weymann fabric body construction technique developed in France, built a total of 13 cars in three styles. Holbrook Company of Hudson, New York, produced seven cars in four versions. One of America's premiere coachbuilders, Brunn & Company in Buffalo, New York, designed and built six cars in four styles. Custom coachbuilders Bohman & Schwartz, which succeeded the Murphy Company in Pasadena, accounted for another nine, but of that number, five were rebodies. Dietrich, Inc. in Detroit built two custom bodies, and Locke & Company of New York produced but a single car. Although there were many "one-off" designs, most of the customs were built in series, the numbers ranging from as few as four to Murphy's record of 53 convertible coupés.

The Model J was available in two wheelbase lengths, $142^{1/2}$ inches and $153^{1/2}$ inches. The only exceptions were the Cooper and Gable cars, which were shortened to 125 inches, and a longer-wheelbase parade car built for evangelist Father Divine.

Throughout the 1930s, American cars were very popular in Europe, and approximately 50 Model J chassis were shipped overseas. Those sent abroad were bodied by Europe's leading *carrosserie*: Gurney Nutting and Barker in England, d'Ieteren Freres and Van den Plas of Belgium, Castagna in Italy, Hermann Graber in

Duesenberg
Model SJ Arlington Torpedo Sedan "Twenty Grand"

Switzerland, and in France, Letourneur et Marchand, Saoutchik, Figoni Falaschi, and Hibbard & Darrin (later Fernandez & Darrin).

The cars bodied in Europe are among the most superbly styled ever to grace the Model J chassis, and today those that survive are among the most highly prized cars from the 1930s.

The majority of foreign-bodied Duesenbergs passed through the Champs Elysées showroom of Motor Deluxe, the Paris dealership of importer E. Z. Sadovich. The prototypical automotive entrepreneur, Sadovich traveled in the right circles, surrounding himself with wealthy industrialists like Antonio Chopieta, who at one time owned five Model J Duesenbergs, including the famous Figoni-bodied French Speedster, owned today by collector Sam Mann.

Sadovich often fronted money for costly coachwork that would eventually be sold to his exclusive clientele, and he personally established the Duesenberg marque in France by entering cars in the Concours d'Elegance at Cannes and Nice and campaigning them in road races across Europe. Sadovich codrove the French Speedster with Prince Nicholas of Romania in the Paris-to-Nice race before selling it to Chopieta in 1931.

A handful of Duesenbergs have become so well-known that they are recognized simply by their names, such as the regal Duesenberg SJ Arlington Torpedo Sedan, better known as the "Twenty Grand." Designed by legendary Duesenberg stylist Gordon Buehrig, the car was bodied in Pasadena by the Walter M. Murphy Company and aptly named for its staggering price in 1933. Built for display at the Chicago Century of

89

Duesenberg
Model J Murphy Dual Cowl Phaeton

Progress World's Fair, it was the most expensive automobile of the year, and today it can be seen on display at the Nethercutt Collection in Sylmar, California.

The most prolific of Duesenberg designs was the Murphy-bodied convertible coupé. This was not only the most popular Duesenberg body style, but one of the best looking, either with the top up or with it lowered and concealed from view beneath a hinged panel on the rear deck. With the top down, the car had the appearance of a true roadster, although it did have wind-up windows in the doors. All of the convertible coupés, with the exception of the two long-wheelbase cars, had rear-hinged doors, and nearly all came with dual side mounts. The factory price was $13,000 in 1930. The rumble seat or luggage deck were extra-cost options. The rarest variation of this design by Murphy was the Torpedo Roadster, shown in a brilliant rose and polished aluminum finish from the collection of William Chorkey.

The increasing depth of the Depression began to take its toll on the company, which found fewer buyers as the 1930s wore on. With declining sales also came the downfall of custom coach-building. By the time Walter M. Murphy closed its doors, the company had produced some of the most spectacular Model J designs of the era, including the Murphy Sport Sedan, which featured a rakish V-frame windshield that widened at the corners and had extremely narrow pillars.

Murphy stylist Franklin Q. Hershey, who penned many of the company's most successful designs and later gained fame as the designer of the 1955 Thunderbird, called it a "Clear-Vision" windshield, a strikingly modern departure from the square-cut lines of most windshields. There were two versions of the Sport Sedan, one with rear quarter windows and another with a solid rear quarter, such as the example pictured from the Dr. Joseph A. Murphy Collection. Both versions featured doors hinged back-to-back with large center-mounted piano-style hinges, another Murphy trait, allowing the rear doors to open conventionally while the fronts unlocked in reverse, or suicide style. Only about seven examples were produced, at a factory price of $13,500.

No other American car, not Lincoln or Packard or even Cadillac, had so powerful an image. Legendary automotive historian Ken Purdy wrote of the Model J and its designer, "Fred Duesenberg had done what is given few men to do; he had chosen a good course and held unswervingly to it. . . . With his mind and his two good hands he had created something new and good and in its way immortal. And the creator is, when all is said and done, the most fortunate of men."

This is the stuff legendary cars are made of, including five of the 100 greatest cars ever built.

1934 DUESENBERG MODEL J MURPHY DUAL COWL PHAETON

Ferrari

166 MM Touring Barchetta

I t wasn't until the late 1940s that American sportsmen began to experience first-hand the joys of driving a Ferrari, principally through former race driver Luigi Chinetti and his Manhattan dealership, the avenue through which Enzo Ferrari's Italian masterpieces passed into the hands of affluent American racing and sports car enthusiasts.

The 166 MM Touring Barchetta is still considered among the Italian automaker's most spectacular models more than 50 years after its debut. The styling of the Barchetta was based in part on the BMW 328 Spyder, designed by Carrozzeria Touring in 1940. All of the Barchetta bodies—of which Touring built some 46 examples —shared the same sleek, swept-back lines, long hood, short rear deck, and ominous grille opening, which was to influence automotive design in Europe, Great Britain, and the United States well into the 1960s.

The 166 Touring Barchetta was the first sports car (as opposed to a race car) ever shown on a Ferrari chassis. The hand-built body was attached to a welded tubular steel framework and then mounted on the Ferrari's short 2,200-mm (86.6-inch) wheelbase. The Superleggera designation on the hood indicated that the car was of Touring's exclusive lightweight construction, for which the Milanese coachbuilder had become renowned. The front suspension was Ferrari's independent A-arm design, supported by a single transverse leaf spring; the rear, a live axle with semielliptical springs and parallel trailing arms on each side. Early Ferraris also used Houdaille hydraulic lever-action-type dampers.

Beneath the long hood was the Colombo-designed 60-degree V-12, an engine as beautifully styled as the body surrounding it. With a displacement of 1,995 cc (122

1950 FERRARI 166 MM TOURING BARCHETTA

cubic inches), output was 140 horsepower at 6,600 rpm. A 60.0-mm (2.362-inch) bore x 58.8-mm (2.315-inch) stroke and a compression ratio of 10:1 were fueled by three Weber 32 DCF twin-choke downdraft carburetors.

As magnificent as the exterior, the Touring designed and built interior featured hand-sewn leather upholstery and trim. Although appointed comparably to a race car, the Touring Barchetta was considered luxurious, or *lusso*, when given the full interior treatment.

The 166 Mille Miglia was arguably the fastest sports car in the world at the time, and with it Scuderia Ferrari's cannonade across Europe recorded more than 80 overall or class victories between April 1948 and December 1953.

In March 1949, Clemente Biondetti won the Targa Florio in a 166 MM, and 166 Inters were first and second in the Coppa Inter-Europa. In April, Biondetti and Bonetto, driving 166 MMs, finished first and second in the Mille Miglia. But it was Chinetti who brought Ferrari its first significant postwar racing victory, codriving a 166 MM Touring Barchetta with Britain's Lord Peter Selsdon in the 1949 Vingt-Quatre Heures du Mans. "Iron Man Chinetti" drove 23 of the 24 hours to clinch Ferrari's first and most important international win. Chinetti went on to win the Spa-Francorchamps 24-hour race for touring cars the following July. In 1950, Alberto Ascari won the Grand Prix du Luxembourg and the Silverstone International Trophy. Dorino Serafini and Luigi Villoresi came in second at Silverstone driving a single-carburetor Barchetta, in all probability the very car pictured in this book, which was sold to Chinetti and later to American driver Bill Spear.

Ferrari
250 GT Spyder California

In 1957, Ferrari's new 250 GT Cabriolet was regarded as an excellent compromise between race car and road car, but *compromise* was never a word that fit well into the Ferrari vocabulary. The mounting dissatisfaction with the 250 GT Cabriolet was truly an ironic turn of events. In the late 1940s, Luigi Chinetti, Enzo Ferrari's long-time friend and U.S. distributor, convinced him that the company needed to produce models that were more comfortable and luxurious than the race-bred sports cars that were then being offered. Ferrari complied, reluctantly. A decade later, it was Chinetti who now complained that Ferrari needed a more sporting open car than the 250 GT Cabriolet. Chinetti wanted a more aggressively styled GT convertible to sell. And his was not the only voice beckoning. Ferrari's West Coast distributor, race driver John von Neumann, was equally disenchanted with the 250 GT Cabriolet. Von Neumann felt that an open car with the characteristics of the lighter, sportier 250 GT Berlinettas would be more successful in the United States. Enzo was persuaded and gave approval for a special series of sports cars to be built, which would be appropriately named the 250 GT Spyder California.

The cars went into limited production in May 1958 and were built through 1960 on the long-wheelbase GT Berlinetta chassis.

The revised coachwork, designed by Sergio Pininfarina, was manufactured in the workshops of Scaglietti, who had become Ferrari's principal coachbuilder. The Spyder California was produced in two series, the long wheelbase, known as the LWB, and the

short wheelbase, SWB, a lighter-weight steel-and aluminum-bodied version introduced in 1960 and produced through 1963.

Intended as a sportier version of the Spyder California, the short-wheelbase model utilized the same chassis design as the 250 GT SWB Berlinetta, offering a wheelbase of only 94.5 inches, lighter overall weight than the LWB Spyder, and the same competent handling characteristics as the competition-bred Berlinettas.

Among a handful of Spyder Californias pressed into competition was a car entered by Luigi Chinetti's North American Racing Team (NART) and driven by Bob Grossman and Ferdinand Tavano to a fifth overall finish at Le Mans in 1959. Several cars were also fitted with competition engines and upon special order supplied with all-aluminum bodies. They were otherwise constructed of steel with aluminum doors and deck lids.

The SWB Spyder California made its debut at the Geneva Salon in March 1960, and these were equipped with new heads and larger valves than the LWB, increasing output to 280 horsepower at 7,000 rpm. (Competition engines were further increased to 300 horsepower with even larger valves, high-lift camshafts, and lighter-weight connecting rods and pistons.) The track was widened on SWB models, which were also the first to switch from lever-type shock absorbers to adjustable telescopic units.

The Spyder California, in either wheelbase, was one of the first Ferrari "driver's cars."

1960 FERRARI 250 GT SPYDER CALIFORNIA

Ferrari
250 GTO

Considered by many to be the most beautiful shape ever to grace an automobile, the Ferrari 250 GTO ("Gran Turismo Omologato") was the quintessential road/race car of the 1960s. The majority of GTO bodies were designed and built for Ferrari by Carrozzeria Scaglietti in Modena, just a few miles down the road from the Ferrari factory. A total of 39 were produced between 1962 and 1964, making this one of Ferrari's rarest and most valuable cars. It would be unusual to see one change hands today for less than $4.5 million!

Essentially a refined version of the 1959–62 short wheelbase 250 GT Berlinetta or SWB, the 250 GTOs were equipped with an improved 3-liter V-12 engine carrying six twin-throat Weber 38DCN carburetors, a five-speed, all-synchromesh gearbox (replacing the four-speed used in the 250 GT SWB), and delivering 300-horsepower output at 8,400 rpm.

In order to be homologated for racing, Ferrari was required by the FIA (Federation Internationale de l-Automobile) to produce 100 examples. At the time he had built fewer than one-third of the cars necessary for homologation. When pressed by the international racing organization as to whether or not he intended to build the rest of the cars, Enzo told them that the market for such a car was already saturated and there were only a few men in the world who could master its ferocity! A bombastic way of telling them no, as only Enzo Ferrari could, and no is no, even in Italian.

Given that the 250 GTO was regarded by the Ferrari factory as merely an improved version of the 250 GT Short Wheelbase Berlinetta, as modified by Giotto Bizzarrini and Sergio Scaglietti in 1961–62, the FIA acquiesced and homologated the car without further question, opening the door for one of history's greatest gran turismos.

In truth, there was some degree of fact to Ferrari's claims, since the GTO chassis was of the same tubular-type construction as the 250 GT SWBs, with an independent front suspension and live rear axle. The basic improvements over the short wheelbase Berlinetta were dry sump lubrication, a new five-speed gearbox, and a more aerodynamic body. It was a thinly disguised lie, but no one dared to challenge the old man.

As expected, the cars were virtually unbeatable, and the 250 GTOs brought Ferrari the coveted Manufacturer's World Championship of sports cars in 1962, 1963, and 1964. A total of 20 first place finishes in 28 races, 15 seconds, and 9 thirds! The car pictured, number 3769, now in a private east coast collection, was raced in France 1962 and 1963 by Fernand Tavano, who usually won, or broke the car trying to.

Of all the celebrated Ferraris built over the past half century, and there have been many, no model has received the universal acclaim of the 250 GTO, a car regarded by collectors the world over as one of the great automobiles of the twentieth century.

Ferrari
275 GTS/4 NART Spyder

Sergio Pininfarina's styling for the Ferrari 275 GTB and GTB/4 combined the better elements of the competition-built 250 GTO, as well as the striking 250 GTB Berlinetta Lusso. The Ferrari stylist's approach was the perfect leitmotif for the new car—a long plunging hood, small oval radiator intake, streamlined covered headlights, pronounced hood bulge, and truncated rear, all perfectly harmonized to the contour of the steeply inclined and sharply curved windshield. The 275 GTB/4 was nothing short of aesthetic classicism, and if the car had any detractors, their only protest was that it too closely resembled the 250 GTO. Hardly a fault.

The GTB/4 proved an incomparable dual-purpose sports car that could challenge the ability of even the most skilled drivers. Says legendary World Driving Champion and former Ferrari factory race driver Phil Hill, "It was like a boulevard version of the GTO."

While there are enthusiasts who will argue the point, the majority will agree that the 275 GTB and GTB/4 were the best-looking Berlinettas ever produced by Ferrari. Of the four-cam models, only about 280 examples were built. The rarest of all 275 GTB/4 models, however, were those *not* produced by Ferrari—at least not directly. They were produced for Ferrari's U.S. importer, Luigi Chinetti, Ferrari's closest friend and the man who helped him rebuild the company after World War II.

Ironically, in his memoirs, *My Terrible Joys,* Enzo Ferrari barely mentions Chinetti's name, yet without him it's unlikely that Ferrari would have had much to write about. History will remember Chinetti, who succumbed to a heart ailment in 1994, shortly after celebrating his 93rd birthday, as the man who truly built the Ferrari legend.

As a dealer and importer, Chinetti understood the American market far better than Ferrari. To please his customers, Luigi would not only challenge Ferrari's

1967 FERRARI 275 GTS/4 NART SPYDER

Ferrari

275 GTB/4

decisions, but at times go out on his own and have special Ferrari models produced at his own expense.

In 1956 he formed the North American Racing Team, better known as NART. It was to be an independent arm of Scuderia Ferrari, which on occasion would also represent the factory when Ferrari decided not to enter events under his own name. Over the years, NART became one of the most illustrious acronyms in American motorsports and a virtual Who's Who of legendary race drivers. Among those who drove for or were discovered by Chinetti were Mario Andretti, Dan Gurney, Paul O'Shea, Richie Ginther, Phil Hill, Stirling Moss, Bob Bondurant, Sam Posey, Jim Kimberly, Brian Redman, and Denise McCluggage. Over the 26-year period between 1956 and 1982, NART campaigned in over 200 races with more than 150 different drivers.

Because of their friendship, Ferrari granted Chinetti the right to use the factory's *Cavallino Rampante* (Prancing Horse) emblem as part of the NART insignia. However, all the decisions regarding the team were Chinetti's, and he often found himself at odds with Ferrari.

They were two very stubborn men, heading at times in the same direction and at others, quite the opposite way. They were, as former race driver and author Denise McCluggage once put it, "Indeed similar. Similar in the way that Yin and Yang are similar. You know, like hills and valleys; you can't have one without the other." The difference was that Chinetti never had the need to stand center stage. "He was perhaps the greatest patron American road racing has ever enjoyed," wrote racing historian Pete Lyons.

Recalls McCluggage, who knew both men very well, "Luigi was more

like the director, always behind the scenes, while Ferrari was grandiose, the grand figure . . . the prototypical operatic tenor."

The development of the NART Spyder in 1967 was the culmination of one of Ferrari and Chinetti's most legendary disagreements. Disapproving of the new Ferrari 275 GTS as a successor to the 250 GT Spyder California, which he had helped create in 1958, Chinetti beseeched Ferrari to build a Spyder version of the 275 GTB/4. Enzo refused. Chinetti's course was clear. His son, Luigi "Coco" Chinetti, Jr., proposed building a Spyder based on the new 275 GTB/4 Berlinetta. To accomplish this, they turned to Sergio Scaglietti, commissioning the *carrozzeria* to remove the roofs from the Berlinettas and build a series of competition Spyders exclusively for Chinetti Motors and NART. Scaglietti was an artist when it came to converting Berlinettas into Spyders, and what emerged from the Modena coachbuilder's palette was a hand-built masterpiece.

Chinetti had selected the greatest Ferrari of its time as the basis for the NART Spyder. Equipped

1968 FERRARI 275 GTB/4

with a four-cam V-12 breathing through six Weber 40 DCN 17 carburetors, and delivering up to 330 horsepower at 8,000 rpm, the 275 GTB/4 was built atop a revised Type 596 all-independently suspended chassis.

From the exterior, the four-cam model was easily distinguished from the standard 275 GTB by a raised central power bulge in the hood. It was also obvious whenever a driver applied substantial pressure to the throttle pedal—the GTB/4 could move from zero-to-60 in 6.7 seconds and reach a top speed in excess of 150 miles per hour. The rebodied Berlinettas were delivered by Scaglietti to Chinetti Motors in Greenwich, Connecticut, and sold exclusively in North America.

The first car arrived stateside in February 1967 and was slated to race at Sebring. Stamped with chassis number 09437, it was painted *giallo solare* (sun yellow), which contrasted with a rich black leather interior. Enzo Ferrari, who had shown little interest in the car, suddenly took offense at the color, telling Chinetti that yellow was not a proper color for a competition car bearing his name. Chinetti, with a sarcastic wit that few could deny, said to Ferrari in his sweetly spoken English dialect, "ProBOBly, the scorers do not miss yellow so easily." Ferrari, in typically dismissive style, glanced over his ever present sunglasses and replied in Italian, "You have made a taxicab." And so, one more little battle of wills had been fought by these two giants, Ferrari the car maker and Chinetti the image maker.

Chinetti entered the first NART Spyder in the 12 Hours of Sebring and selected two women to drive, Pinkie Rollo and automotive journalist and professional race driver Denise McCluggage. Despite an electrical problem and an overly long pit stop for a tire change, the NART Spyder still managed to finish 17th overall, the single Ferrari survivor among a field that had included seven at the start.

Following Sebring, Chinetti gave the car a complete overhaul and a new paint job—this time a deep burgundy—and sent it off to *Road & Track* magazine for testing. The article appearing in the September 1967 issue reported an impressive top speed of 155 miles per hour and the velocity at the end of a 14.7-second standing start quarter-mile as 99 miles per hour. *R&T* proclaimed it "The most satisfying sports car in the world." After the road test, the car was delivered to the movie set of Steve McQueen's new film, *The Thomas Crown Affair*. Although it was only briefly featured in the 1968 thriller, McQueen, an impassioned sports car enthusiast and accomplished race driver, was so taken with the NART Spyder that he purchased car number 10453 from Chinetti. The car pictured is the original NART driven by McCluggage and featured in *The Thomas Crown Affair*.

Although only nine examples were built, among Ferraris it is a respectable number, especially for a car that the factory had no intention of making. Fortunately, thanks to Luigi Chinetti's vision of a proper Spyder, today we have the 275 GTS/4, truly one of the 100 greatest cars.

The 1968 Ferrari 275 GTB/4 Berlinetta is from the Bruce Meyer Collection. The NART Spyder was formerly owned by Symbolic Motor Car Company in La Jolla, California, and is now in a private collection.

Ferrari
Dino 206 GT

The Dino is very much a part of Ferrari lore, even though technically it is not a Ferrari, since the engines were built by Fiat.

In a very loose interpretation, the Dino is to Ferrari what the 914 was to Porsche—a less expensive companion model, but to Enzo Ferrari the reasons for producing the Dino were very personal. The high-performance V-6 models were produced to commemorate Ferrari's son, Dino, who died in 1956.

Dino Ferrari had suffered from muscular dystrophy since birth but had much of his father's will. He managed to get through school and acquire a degree in engineering, but as his health began to fail he was forced to spend most of his time in bed. Enzo and his close friend Vittorio Jano, one of Italy's greatest automotive engineers, would spend time with Dino in his room, discussing the young Ferrari's ideas for a 1.5-liter racing engine. Dino had even written a two-part thesis on the design of a high-performance V-6 engine, which was published in the Italian magazine *Velocita*.

Writing about Dino in his memoirs, Enzo said that "For reasons of mechanical efficiency [Dino] had finally come to the conclusion that the engine should be a V-6 and we accepted his decision." Five months after Dino passed away, Ferrari created the 156 Dino engine.

Dino's inevitable death still came as a blow to Enzo, and to honor Dino's memory he proceeded to develop an entire line of Dino engines over a 10-year period, for Formula 1, Formula 2, sports racing, and GT road cars.

Pininfarina bodied the first Dino road car to be powered by a rear-mounted V-6. The prototype, known as the Dino 206 GT Speciale, was displayed at the Paris Motor Show in October 1965. A second version, called the Dino Berlinetta GT, was displayed at the 1966 Turin Motor Show. As in the earlier example, the engine was positioned longitudinally ahead of the rear axle. A third and final version made its debut

1968 FERRARI DINO 206 GT

at Turin in November 1967, this one with the Fiat-produced engine mounted transversely and built in unit with a five-speed transaxle. An additional prototype was shown in Brussels the following year, and early in 1969 body production was started at Carrozzeria Scaglietti in Modena. By the end of the year roughly 150 Dinos had been built, all with aluminum bodies.

The 206 GT was the first production Ferrari to be given only even chassis numbers (road cars had, with few exceptions, been serialized in odd number only) and the first to bear neither the yellow *Cavallino Rampante* emblem nor the Ferrari name. It simply bore the signature *Dino GT*.

The majority of first series Dinos were sold in Italy and Europe, although a few were brought to the United States in 1969 by Luigi Chinetti. The 206 GT was replaced in 1969 by the 246 GT, which remained in production through 1973. The 246 GTS, featuring a removable targa-type roof panel, was added in 1972 and concluded Dino production in 1974.

The Dino became one of Ferrari's most popular and affordable models and the inspiration for numerous cars of similar styling for more than 20 years. The Dino is regarded as one of designer Sergio Pininfarina's greatest styling achievements, but to Enzo Ferrari, each was a monument to his fallen son.

1968 FERRARI DINO 206 GT

Ferrari
365 GTB/4 Daytona Spyder

Berlinetta and *Spyder* are two of the most important words in the language of Ferrari, words that define the essence of the automobile. The same was meant to be for the 365 GTB/4 Daytona Berlinetta and Spyder, cars that for many Ferrari collectors have become the definitive examples of the differing design strategies.

Since Ferrari first began offering road cars in the late 1940s, the Berlinetta design had evolved into one of Maranello's most popular body styles for both road and competition cars. Ferrari styling had for years dictated that every car have a dynamic oval grille, a pronounced, aggressive visage that had characterized Ferrari design since the days of the 166 MM Touring Barchettas. For the Daytona, however, designer Sergio Pininfarina and his staff were about to take a detour, departing from all previous models and abandoning for the first time the traditional Ferrari hallmark. Pininfarina was convinced that aerodynamics would prove as important to the new Ferrari's performance as its suspension and engine.

Surrendering the aggressive oval grille design and high-crowned fenders presented one unique challenge to Pininfarina: where to place the headlights, which had for more than 20 years been a part of the fender design. With the 365 GTB/4 there were no front fenders, at least not in a classic sense. This brief impasse led to the most dramatic styling change in Ferrari history.

For the 365 GTB/4, Pininfarina chose to set paired headlamps slightly back from the nose of the car and wrap the entire front end with a single band of transparent plastic. This nose band—a sheet of Perspex approximately eight inches high—was then carried around the front corners of the car to integrate parking and side marker light units, ending just short of the front wheel arches. The inner surface of the Perspex was painted black except for the very center,

left clear to display the rectangular Ferrari emblem attached to the bodywork underneath.

There was a decidedly rakish angle to the Daytona's roofline, establishing a fast-back appearance at the rear of the body before angling down to the decklid and an extremely large and almost flat rear window, providing the Daytona with something few Ferrari owners had ever seen, a view out the back of the car!

Ironically, the car's most attractive feature, the Perspex-covered headlights, became its greatest handicap when Ferrari tried to sell the Daytonas in the United States, because they were not in accordance with federal height requirements. Ferrari found it necessary to design a second front end for export, which positioned iodine headlamps in a retractable housing that mimicked the Perspex nose when the lights were off and popped up (Corvette style) when they were turned on, at which point the entire aerodynamic theory of the Daytona's front end design was shot.

The new 60-degree double overhead cam V-12 powering the Daytona was derived from earlier designs by Gioacchino Colombo and Aurelio Lampredi. Displacing 4.4 liters (268 cubic inches) and teamed with six Weber DCN 20 twin-barrel 40-mm downdraft carburetors, the fed-legal Ferrari engine delivered 352 horsepower at 7,500 rpm, taking the drive through a ZF all-synchromesh five-speed transaxle built-in unit with the differential.

Following the 275 GTB/4, which had preceded it, the Daytona had a four-wheel independent suspension comprised of unequal length A-arms with tubular shock absorbers, coil springs, and front and rear antiroll bars. The Daytonas were also equipped with Dunlop ventilated disc brakes on all four wheels.

At the time of its introduction in 1968, the 365 GTB/4 Berlinetta was the

most expensive and fastest road car in Ferrari's 21-year history. Priced at just under $20,000, the Daytona was capable of reaching a top speed of 174 miles per hour according to factory tests.

Following the Daytona Berlinetta's introduction, work was begun on a Spyder version to be introduced in 1969. Although building Spyders was something of a tradition with Ferrari, beheading the 365 GTB/4 flew in the face of reason. Designed to take advantage of Europe's high-speed auto routes, it was the most aerodynamic model in Ferrari's stable. If the roof was removed, all of the aerodynamic gains

would be gone with the wind! Making a Daytona Spyder was not logical, counseled Pininfarina. Of course, who said logic has anything to do with convertibles?

"In Europe, we are accustomed to thinking of a sports car as a Berlinetta. On the contrary, a sports car for an American many times means a Spyder," says the car's legendary designer. In all, 1,383 Daytonas were produced, including 122 Spyders, 96 of which were sold to customers in, you guessed it, the United States.

The car pictured is the Daytona Spyder prototype produced in 1969. It presently resides in a private collection.

1969 FERRARI 365 GTB/4 DAYTONA SPYDER

Ford Model T

Carl Benz may have patented the first automobile in 1886, but Henry Ford put the world on wheels in 1909 with the Model T, the most important American car of the twentieth century. "Instead of spending all your life on the farm you actually got into town and, in fact, traveled around to other states. Everybody loved the automobile in America," says former General Motors director of design David Holls, "and that love affair started with the Model T."

Up until Ford established the moving assembly line, and managed to cut production costs, the average automobile sold for $1,000 while some were two to three times that amount. The '09 Model T started at just $825 and by 1912 had dropped to only $590. By 1917 the cost of tooling had long since been amortized and the Ford Motor Company lowered the base price of a Model T to $345 for the two-passenger runabout. Almost anyone could afford a Ford, including Ford employees, who earned the highest wages in the auto industry, $5 a day.

Model T body styles ranged from the basic two-passenger runabout to sedans, coupes, phaetons, and town cars, the most elaborate and expensive of which sold for just $645 in 1917.

Over the years, Henry Ford had been frugal with his engineering, making necessary changes but always being mindful of the pragmatic attributes of the Model T: affordability, ease of operation with a reliable, easily maintained four-cylinder engine, and discreet styling. At least that's how Henry saw it. What he didn't see was everyone else passing him by. Left to his own devices he would have continued building the Model T into the 1930s, although by 1924 the base price had been reduced to just $290, making it the most affordable car in the world, and at that price Henry may have been right.

Although the Model T had been redesigned several times over the years to keep pace with contemporary styling, they were far from modern by late 1920s

1911 FORD MODEL T

Ford Model A

standards. The Model T had been in production for almost 19 years. After building more than 20 million cars in the United States, Canada, and Europe, Ford assembled the last Tin Lizzie in June 1927.

Ford shut down his production facilities from June to mid-October to make the change over to the all-new 1928 Model A, what was perhaps the most highly anticipated automobile in American history. Ford dealers papered over their windows, and on the day the cars were announced, December 2, 1927, there were lines a city block long outside Ford showrooms and crowds so thick police had to be called in to direct traffic. It was an event unlike any before, and the Model A was an instant success. In the first year Ford delivered a staggering 888,059 and in 1929 Model A sales topped the million mark, making Ford the bestselling car in America, with a base price starting at just $460 for a four-door phaeton.

Like the Model T, the Model A used a four-cylinder engine developing a modest 40 horsepower, sufficient to propel the cars to a top speed of 60 mph, and competitive enough in price and performance to keep Chevrolet and Dodge at bay.

By 1930 Ford had 32 assembly plants operating in the United States, 3 in Canada, and 10 in the rest of the world. But even Henry Ford wasn't immune to the Great Depression, and in 1932 sales tumbled to 232,125 cars, posting a loss for Ford Motor Company of $74 million. Part of the loss, however, was in developmental cost for a new engine to power the Model A's replacement, the '32 Ford V-8, which made its debut on March 31, beginning yet another chapter in Ford history.

Although there have been many great cars in Ford's 96-year history, the Model T and Model A will always be the two most significant to come from Ford Motor Company, wondrous and remarkable automobiles that have left an indelible mark on the highways of the world.

Ford Super Deluxe

"Woodie" Wagon

Wood, perhaps the most versatile and enduring medium in history, has played a role in almost every facet of life since the beginning of time. Wood for fuel, to keep the glow of mankind's primordial fire alive, wood from which to create utensils and tools, to build the wheel, the cart, the carriage, and ultimately the framework of an automobile.

It is a substance as strong as steel, when need be, and as fragile as Limoges in the hands of a woodworker crafting the veneer fascia of an instrument panel. Wood has played many roles throughout the history of automobiles, and in the late 1930s and early postwar 1940s, it was the cornerstone of an entire generation of cars known today as "Woodies."

Among Detroit's Big Three, Ford was the first to go into postwar production, introducing its new models in 1945. Full station wagon production began only three months after the war had ended, with Ford and Mercury once again sharing the same body styles—which remained basically unchanged from 1942.

With only a few exceptions, station wagon bodies were built by independent contractors, mostly furniture makers. Among the companies supplying them to General Motors and Chrysler were J. T. Cantrell, Mid-State Body, U.S. Body & Forging, Hercules, and Ypsilanti Furniture, manufacturer of the Ionia body.

The wood used for the Ionia was maple and mahogany, and the workmanship that went into each was equal to that in the finest home furnishings produced by Ypsilanti. Each station wagon was nothing short of furniture on wheels—an art long since replaced by wood-grained decals, photoengravings, and appliqués.

Ford, unlike many of its competitors, built a number of its own wood bodies, using ash and maple harvested from the company-owned timber mill at Iron Mountain, in Michigan's upper peninsula.

Like so many automakers, Ford's early postwar models employed the same basic

1947 FORD SUPER DELUXE "WOODIE" WAGON

styling seen in those produced in 1941 and 1942. The most significant change on the Fords was redesigned grillework on both the Deluxe and Super Deluxe. Red striping detail in the grille design of 1946 Fords also set them apart from the later 1947–48 models, which had plain radiator grille bars. They were further distinguished by the different shape and location of the parking lamps, moved from above the grille in '46 to below the headlights in '47 and '48. Other notable changes included the design of the hood ornament, width of the body and fender moldings, and a large bright-metal nameplate on the rear decklid of 1947–48 models, replacing the two chrome strips used on 1946 Fords.

For 1947, Ford continued to manufacture its Woodie wagons in both a Deluxe and a Super Deluxe version. The Super Deluxe model pictured sold for $1,975. Differentiating the '47 Deluxe and Super Deluxe was the lighter-colored exterior-door wood used on Deluxe models and the richer-textured dark wood used on the Super, along with upgraded upholstery and trim. The dash panels in both models were metal, painted with a maplewood grain finish.

A tremendous amount of wood was used in building the wagons, particularly the headliners, with long white ash slats lining the interior roof. The inside door panels were mahogany and the outside panels a combination of mahogany and birch. The well-sprung and heavily padded front and rear seats in the Ford models were upholstered in smooth tan leather, while the Mercury version offered buyers a choice of tan, red, or gray leather.

The outstanding 1946–48 Ford and Mercury station wagons would be the last of the full wood-bodied types produced, indicative of Ford's fabled Iron Mountain craftsmanship. By 1949, the cars were becoming too expensive to build.

A decade later, the Woodie became the California Dreamin' car, the subject of songs by Jan and Dean and the Beach Boys, and the ideal of every surfer boy and girl. Most surfer Woodies were either Fords or Mercurys. Many fell under the saw in the '60s to accommodate more surfboards, while others simply fell victim to rotting wood and the elements. Today, totally restored Woodies such as this '47 Ford owned by Brad Smith, are a rare find.

The Ford Woodie wagon has become one of the few models in the history of the automobile that is uniquely American.

1947 FORD SUPER DELUXE "WOODIE" WAGON

Ford Thunderbird

In 1952, a total of 11,199 new sports cars were registered in the United States, a paultry 0.27 percent of car registrations. A year later, speaking before the Society of Automotive Engineers, Zora Arkus-Duntov said, "Considering the statistics, the American public does not want a sports car at all. But do the statistics give a true picture? As far as the American market is concerned, it is still an unknown quantity, since an American sports car catering to American tastes, roads, way of living, and national character has not yet been on the market." Prophetic words from the man who would make the Corvette legendary in the late 1950s and throughout the 1960s. In 1953, however, the Chevrolet Corvette was not that kind of car.

A year prior to the Corvette's introduction, one of chief designer Frank Hershey's assistants at Ford brought him a bootlegged picture of the proposed Corvette sports car being developed across town at GM. Hershey, who had designed some of the greatest cars of the 1930s, including many of the legendary Duesenberg bodies, immediately began a crash program to develop a competitive model. Hershey and his staff, Damon Woods and L. David Ash, had it roughed out in only a few weeks. Thanks to Hershey's initiative, the exterior lines were completed before Ford management even realized they were going to need a sports car.

The excitement surrounding the Corvette's public debut at the GM Motorama in New York was largely due to its sleek, futuristic appearance and unique Fiberglas body. For Ford and Hershey, it was fortunate that the Corvette came out first. It allowed them to learn from Chevrolet's mistakes. And there were plenty. GM management had misinterpreted the popularity of the MG and Jaguar XK–120, cars that appealed to a very small segment of car buyers. The Corvette was styled to appeal to sports car enthusiasts but engineered for the general consumer. Thus it appealed to neither. Once the novelty wore off and the first few hundred were sold, Corvette sales tumbled into 1954 and all but stalled in 1955 when the Thunderbird came out. Americans wanted the styling alright, but they had come to expect roll-up windows, a big V-8, and choices like a hardtop or

convertible, an automatic or a manual transmission. The Corvette offered few of these options.

Hershey was quick to recognize the Corvette's shortcomings, and when the Thunderbird came to market in the fall of 1954, it had an easily operated convertible top plus a removable hardtop, roll-up windows, and a powerful V-8 engine under the hood. Ford called it a "Personal Luxury Car." Chevrolet called it trouble.

Mechanically, the Thunderbird would be everything the Corvette was not. High on the list was Chevrolet's failure to give the car substantial performance. Ford answered with a new overhead valve "Y-block" V-8 engine displacing 292 cubic inches and coupled to either a manual gearbox or Ford-O-Matic transmission. The four-barrel carburetor-fed 292 delivered 193 horsepower through the manual gears and 198 horsepower with the automatic.

Built on a 102-inch wheelbase, front and rear track measured 56 inches, overall length was 175.2 inches, and width 70.3 inches. The suspension was Ford's new independent coil spring Ball-Joint front and leaf spring rear.

Everyone at Ford had done their job well, from Hershey's designers to the engineering department and marketing, and the American public took notice by purchasing 16,155 Thunderbirds the first year, better than four times the number of Corvettes sold in 1955.

For 1956 Ford made numerous changes in the Thunderbird, but the most famous were the introduction of the porthole top and the Continental spare. Engine output was increased with an optional 312-cubic-inch V-8, developing 225 horsepower.

The big changes came in 1957, with a new front grille and bumper design that incorporated the bumper guards and turn indicators. The rear quarter panels received a redo, with fins extending from just behind the door handles to the totally restyled tail-lights. Pacing the rest of the 1957 Ford changes, the standard engine was updated to deliver 245 horsepower, and the Thunderbird received a new dashboard design.

By midyear the Thunderbird was developing into America's number one sports car, despite Chevrolet's excellent restyling of the '57 Corvette and new fuel-injected V-8 engine. Both were now true enthusiasts' cars. To rankle Chevrolet, Ford produced 208 Thunderbirds in 1957 equipped with 300-horsepower McCulloch-supercharged engines, just to better the Corvette's new 283-horsepower V-8.

A performance battle was beginning to take shape between Ford and Chevrolet, but it was over almost before it began. Ford's new division manager Robert S. McNamara (later Secretary of Defense under Presidents Kennedy and Johnson), who took over just as the 1957 models were being finalized, decided that in 1958 the Thunderbird would become a large, four-passenger luxury car.

The 1955 and 1956 Thunderbirds had been very successful, with sales totaling over 32,000 for the first two model years, and when word got out that the two-seater was going out of production, so many orders poured in for the '57 T-Bird that Ford actually had to extend the production run. The last 1957s were being built concurrently with the first 1958 four-seaters just to meet demand!

Four decades later, the 1955 to 1957 Thunderbirds are still in demand and one of the most popular American cars ever built.

Ford Shelby

"Flip-Top" Cobra & 427 Cobra

The year was 1959, and a tall, lanky Texan named Carroll Shelby had become only the second American race car driver in history to win the 24 Hours of LeMans. Unfortunately, Shelby's racing career, which had begun behind the wheel of an MG TC in 1952, was about to be cut short by a heart that lacked the strength of the man's ambitions. During the grueling 24-hour event, Shelby had been taking nitroglycerin tablets to ease the angina pains wracking his chest as he manhandled his Aston-Martin around the demanding 8.47-mile Circuit de la Sarthe. After the 1960 season, the doctors told Shelby it was time to retire. Five years later, the man who had earned a reputation for his aggressive driving style and colorfully laced language had gone from race car driver to race car builder, and won the World Manufacturer's Championship for Ford.

Having been turned away by General Motors in 1962 when he suggested putting an American V-8 under the hood of a British-built AC Ace roadster, Shelby ended up on Ford's doorstep that same year through a mere twist of fate. He found his way via help from *Hot Rod* magazine editor Ray Brock, and, to his surprise, the Dearborn automaker was willing to give his idea a shot. The company was coming out of what former executive Rey Geddes, later to become a principal in the Shelby-Ford relationship, once called "the MacNamara era."

In the late 1950s, Robert S. MacNamara (later to become Secretary of Defense under Presidents Kennedy and Johnson) had turned Ford around financially at the cost of quality and creativity. Among other things, he had killed the two-seat Thunderbird. When Lee Iacocca was appointed vice president and general manager of the Ford Division in November 1960, he brought a sudden awareness of racing, and the youth market in particular, which Ford had long since abandoned. At the same time, Henry Ford II announced that he "wouldn't be opposed to a factory

racing program in full public view"—this in spite of the official Automobile Manufacturer's Association ban on factory-supported racing, an agreement every American automaker had signed and was clandestinely breaking by providing support to privately owned race teams. Carroll Shelby had arrived at absolutely the right moment.

Geddes, a lawyer and financial analyst for Ford, flew out to California to see what Shelby had accomplished with the 289 V-8 and AC roadster. He slipped behind the wheel of the refined two-seater and almost drove it into a telephone pole. It was fast, "went like stink," said Shelby. "Left Geddes pretty damned impressed"—enough so that he recommended that Ford set up Shelby Enterprises as a separate company, providing dealers, engines, technical assistance, and, most important, financing to get the operation up and running as quickly as possible. It was the dawn of an era that would add a new chapter to the history of the American automobile.

After a short time working out of Lance Reventlow's race facility in Venice, California, Shelby and Ford leased two aircraft hangars at Los Angeles International Airport in the fall of 1964 and converted them into the first Cobra assembly line.

The 289 Cobras were formidable competitors in the hands of drivers like Dave MacDonald and Ken Miles, but Shelby had an even more powerful car waiting in the wings—the 427 Cobra.

Something of a revolutionary design, the 427 prototype was done at around the same time as the pictured CSX 2196, an experimental Cobra built in August 1964 by Ken Miles, Bill Eaton, and Joe Fukashima. It was designed to accommodate a special aluminum Ford NASCAR 390-cubic-inch V-8. Capable of developing nearly 500 horsepower, its mission was simple: to demolish Zora Arkus-Duntov's Corvette Grand Sports at Nassau in 1964.

During the previous year's International Bahamas Speed Week, Duntov's Corvettes had beaten the 289 Shelbys, giving the team its first all-out defeat at the hands of Chevrolet. The Cobras had lost before by breaking, but they had never been outrun. The 390 was to be the instrument of Shelby's revenge.

Known as the "Flip-Top Cobra," or "Flip-Top Box," the design, conceived by Miles, called for cantilevered front and rear body sections divided by the driver's compartment. The nose, hood, and front fenders were completed as one section and hinged at the front; trunk and rear fenders finished as a single piece and hinged at the rear, allowing easy access from either end to the car's inner workings. "Weighing only sixteen hundred pounds," said Shelby, "that somebitch went like a rocket down the straightaway!"

Unfortunately, Ford's experimental engine was not as good as the car Shelby had built for it. The 390 proved to be extremely short on reliability. After leaving the Corvettes half a mile behind on the first lap, the engine expired midway thorough the Tourist Trophy Race, ending Ken Miles's onslaught and leaving the door wide open for Roger Penske's Chevrolet. The car had, however, proven its point. When it ran, it was faster than the Corvettes. Another 390 was put into the Flip-Top, and it was entered in the Governors Trophy Race, but that engine failed as well. When the CSX 2196 was returned to Shelby American, it was refitted with a 427.

Often thought to be the 427 prototype, it was actually built concurrently with the 427 test car raced by Ken Miles at Sebring in March 1964. The Flip-Top has survived almost intact for 35 years and is now restored to its original Guardsman Blue color scheme and resides in a private collection.

Among Cobras, this is the most famous snake that Carroll Shelby ever uncoiled.

Ford Mustang

I t was really a 1965 model, but Ford made a point of introducing the car on April 17, 1964, to totally catch the cross-town competition (read: General Motors) completely off guard and also to qualify it as the official pace car for the 1964 Indianapolis 500.

It is laughable now, but, in 1964, GM management was scarcely moved by Ford's new 2 + 2 sports model, believing, and we kid you not, that they already had a worthy competitor in the Chevrolet Corvair! GM changed its tune after Ford sold 400,000 Mustangs in the first full year of production, making it the bestselling new car in history. This, of course, explains GM's rush to production with the 1967 Chevrolet Camaro.

The first Mustangs were available in three body styles: hardtop coupé, convertible, and fastback. Ford's pony car theme extended from the grille emblem, a galloping Mustang, to the herd of horses running pell-mell across the deluxe seatback upholstery.

The Mustang's body styling was as trendsetting as the very notion of the car, introducing what would come to be known industrywide as the long hood–short rear deck design, copied over the years by virtually every automaker in the world.

The car made popular such features as bucket seats and a standard center console-mounted shifter, offered with a choice of three transmissions (two manual gear boxes and one automatic) and three engines: a 120-horsepower six-cylinder; a 260-cubic-inch, 164-horsepower V-8 (replaced late in 1964 by a 200-horsepower 289); or a 289-cubic-inch, 210-horsepower V-8 (later replaced by a 225-horsepower four-barrel 289). Beginning in June 1964, a high-performance 289 option, developing 271 horsepower, was added as the top-of-the-line model, giving buyers a full range of styles and performance options from which to choose.

The success of the car over the past 35 years speaks for itself. Few automobiles in the latter half of this century have been as consequential as the Ford Mustang—one car that truly did make a difference.

1964¹ᐟ² FORD MUSTANG

Ford Shelby Mustang G.T. 350

The 1965 Shelby G.T. 350 was exactly the car aficionados had hoped the original Mustang would be, but building a car for the mass market precluded anything so performance-oriented. As a Shelby Mustang, however, more power and Cobra-like handling were to be expected. Said Shelby, "Shucks, it wasn't nothin' 'cept to take a darn good car an' make it even goodern."

To make the stock Mustang "goodern," Shelby ordered cars with just about everything removed, from the wheel covers and grille bars to the hood and springs. Shelby American rebuilt the engines and suspensions, changed the hood, nose, and grille, and painted all of the 1965 cars white with two wide Guardsman Blue racing stripes running from nose to tail. All G.T. 350s had black interiors and came with a special instrument pod in the middle of the dashboard housing a tachometer and oil pressure gauge.

Ford's goal was to have a car that could be raced in SCCA Production Category B amateur racing. To do this Shelby boosted the 289's output to 306 horsepower with an aluminum Cobra high-rise intake manifold, 715-cfm Holley center-pivot float carburetor, finned aluminum Cobra valve covers, an extra-capacity aluminum oil pan, and Tri-Y exhaust headers. Note that to allow the engine to breathe easier and develop a throatier exhaust glasspacked bullet mufflers were used with exhaust pipes exiting just in front of the rear wheels.

The suspension was stiffened with stabilizer bars, lowered upper "A" arms, Koni shocks, and rear traction bars. The underhood area was also strengthened with a one-piece export-type brace attached to both shock absorber towers and the firewall. The end result was a car that road hard, drove hard, and as Shelby said, "went like stink." In 1966, Shelby added six G.T. 350 convertibles to the production run, and the example pictured is Carroll Shelby's personal car.

1966 FORD SHELBY MUSTANG G.T. 350

Ford Shelby Mustang G.T. 500

Ford had started a revolution in the American automotive industry with the 1964½ Mustang, the most successful new car the company had introduced since the Model A. But success is fleeting, and Lee Iacocca had a better idea—a second version of the Mustang for out-and-out performance enthusiasts. And he had the man to build it—Carroll Shelby.

The G.T. 500 was the second Shelby Mustang concoction, this one taking a page from the Cobra era when race driver Ken Miles and Carroll Shelby first shoehorned a 427 NASCAR-ized engine under the bonnet of a 289 Cobra. With that in mind, Carroll decided to up the performance ante on the new 1967 Shelby Mustangs by adding a 428-cubic-inch V-8 as a companion model to the earlier 289 V-8–powered G.T. 350.

Surrounded by a new, stockier, even more menacing Shelby-styled Mustang body, the new G.T. 500 came packing an engine called the Cobra LeMans, a "street" cousin to the 427s used by Shelby to win the legendary 24 Hours. The 428 was a passenger car engine—quieter, less temperamental, and nearly $1,000 cheaper than the 427 but it was not by any means tame, developing 355 horsepower, delivered posthaste by a four-speed transmission and positraction rear end. It was basically the same engine used in the Thunderbird and Police Interceptor cars. Equipped with hydraulic valve lifters, the 428 breathed through two Holley 600 four-barrel carburetors and could punch its way to 60 mph in 6.5 seconds, through the quarter mile in 15.5 seconds, and to a top speed of 132 mph.

G.T. 500s started life as Mustangs, stripped of their front and rear sheetmetal,

engine, and trunk lids at Shelby American's Los Angeles facility. In their place went fiberglass panels stylized by Ford's Chuck McHose and Shelby American. The result was an aggressive nose, arching three inches farther forward than the stock Mustang's, forming a deep cowling for the headlights and recessed driving lights, which were positioned inside the G.T. 500's massive grille opening. The Shelby hood was a true piece of work, a bodybuilder's set of air scoops sweeping back from the edge of the nose to the cowl, giving the front end of the G.T. 500 an appearance ferocious enough to swallow up whatever got in its way. The view most other drivers got, however, was of the Shelby's back end, fitted with a wide Kamm-type rear deck treatment and spoiler and two sets of Shelby-ized taillight lenses spreading the full width of the body and divided by a Shelby fuel cap with Cobra insignia.

More manageable than the quirky G.T. 350, the G.T. 500 was what *Car and Driver* described in its February 1967 issue as "an adult sports car." It was also the first production car to come factory equipped with a real built-in roll bar and shoulder harnesses.

The G.T. 500 may have been a larger, more luxurious, smoother-riding Shelby than the G.T. 350, but it was still a Cobra at heart, with a high-performance tuned suspension and five-spoke alloy wheels wrapped with low-profile Goodyear E-70-15 tires.

With a lofty price in 1967 of $5,043, the G.T. 500 wasn't for everyone, but it was right for Carroll Shelby, who announced, "This is the first car I'm really proud of."

The 1968 models, such as this striking red G.T. 500 from the Tom Reddington collection, were modestly restyled with an even more aggressive front end featuring wider hood scoops and a lower valance opening to further enlarge the size of the grille. Lucas fog lamps were mounted inside the grille, and Shelby was spelled out across the nose of the car. Under the '68 G.T. 500 hood was the latest 360-horse-power version 428 Ford Police Interceptor V-8.

In 1968 production of the Shelby Mustangs moved from the Shelby American facility in Los Angeles to the A. O. Smith Company in Livonia, Michigan. The Shelby line continued in production through 1970, bringing an end to one of the greatest high-performance eras in Ford history.

125

Hispano-Suiza H6B

A mong the great European classics of the 1930s, the Hispano-Suiza is considered one of the finest cars of its time, with a history dating back to the 1890s. It was during the late 1920s and up until 1937, when the company ended automobile production in France, that the Sociedad Hispano-Suiza Fabrica de Automoviles built its greatest cars.

Often considered French cars, Hispano-Suizas are actually of Spanish origin. Under the direction of the brilliant Swiss automotive engineer Marc Birkigt, the firm prospered through several owners, two reorganizations, and the relocation of its primary automotive production to Paris beginning in 1911. The original factories in Barcelona and Madrid also built cars throughout the company's history, but the most prominent models bearing the Hispano-Suiza name and flying stork emblem were to come from France.

Those whose interests include vintage aircraft may recognize the Hispano-Suiza name more readily than do automotive enthusiasts. The development and manufacturing of aircraft engines—among the best ever built—was the company's principal business and the ultimate cause of the French division's demise. Converted to manufacture V-12 aero engines at the beginning of World War II, the Paris automotive factory was confiscated by the Germans when they invaded France. The remaining factories in Spain continued to produce cars up until 1944.

Among the company's greatest designs was the 1919 H6 and its subsequent development into the H6B and H6C Sport, or Boulogne, model. All were powered by an overhead-cam light-alloy six-cylinder engine, which evolved from the Hispano-Suiza aircraft engine in 1918 and was so well engineered that it would remain in production from the end of World War I until the early 1930s. In its latter form, the H6C engine displaced a massive 7.9 liters, or 479.2 cubic inches. The H6C models were capable of attaining speeds in excess of 100 mph, at the time the highest speed imaginable in a passenger car.

Hispano-Suiza J12

Considered the best-built automobiles in Europe and commensurately priced several thousand dollars higher than a Rolls-Royce Silver Ghost or Phantom, Hispano-Suizas were regarded with the highest esteem by everyone from General Motors' chief stylist Harley Earl (who copied Hispano-Suiza styling for the 1927 LaSalle, right down to a version of the flying stork hood ornament!) to artist Pablo Picasso, the Rothschilds, and many of the wealthiest families on two continents.

In 1931, Birkigt launched the company into the multicylinder wars by doubling the capacity of the Hispano-Suiza engine, creating the most expensive car in the organization's history, the J12, powered by a massive 9,424-cc V-12 engine, producing 200 horsepower at 3,000 rpm. Later models equipped with a high-performance crankshaft increased output to a staggering 250 horsepower. A J12 was capable of reaching a top speed in excess of 110 miles per hour and could clip the distance from zero-to-60 in just 12 seconds.

Only 100 J12s were produced through 1937, each with coachwork by the leading design houses on both sides of the Atlantic.

This handsome 1922 H6B Cabriolet deVille from the Nethercutt Collection was bodied by Paris coachbuilder Jacques Saoutchik. The car's superbly proportioned bodylines and luxurious interior commanded an equally impressive price in 1928, the astounding sum of $15,000. The equally striking 1933 J12 Coupe deVille, also from the Nethercutt Collection and bodied in Paris by Binder, features a removable hardtop, allowing it to become an open car in summer and a closed car in less seasonable weather. The elegant and powerful J12 models earned Hispano-Suiza the moniker "Queen of the Road" and an irrefutable rank in the history of great automobiles.

Hudson Hornet Convertible

T here's nothing to compare with the sounds of a convertible: the tires singing their song as they roll ribbons of pavement into fleeting images in the rearview mirror, the rush of wind surging over the windshield, the mechanical chant of the engine and the burbling of the exhaust pipes filling the air. In the postwar Fifties, this was driving at its absolute best, and few cars made it more enjoyable than a Hudson Hornet, America's leading high-performance champion. Hudson? Believe it or not, in the 1950s Hudsons cleaned just about everyone's clock in AAA and NASCAR competition!

From the very beginning, Hudsons were known for their performance. At Daytona Beach in April 1916, a Hudson set the one-mile straightaway stock car speed record at 102.5 mph In May at Sheepshead Bay, a Hudson took the 24-hour stock car record at a 74.8-mph average, a mark that would go unbroken for 15 years. And it was a Hudson that set the world's first double transcontinental record, driving from San Francisco to New York and back in September 1916.

It was no surprise to those who knew Hudson's history that the Hornet burst upon the post–World War II automotive scene and found almost immediate celebrity in AAA and NASCAR racing. From 1951 through 1954, Hudson Hornets won more stock car races and more season championships under AAA and NASCAR auspices than any other American make. And, mind you, this was accomplished with an in-line six-cylinder engine competing against the best new V-8s that GM, Ford, and Chrysler had to offer!

Victory in showroom stock, of course, did not always guarantee showroom sales, and by late 1953 Hudson was facing the reality of declining market share and the

probability of a merger with Nash in order to survive. But even as Hudson's star was dimming, the company managed to produce the Hornet, one of the truly great postwar American cars.

Introduced in 1951, the sporty Hudson models were offered in four different body styles: a sleek four-door Sedan; a two-door Club Coupe (a favorite for racing); a two-door Convertible Brougham, such as this beautifully restored example from the Nethercutt Collection; and the slick two-door Hollywood Hardtop, the glamour car of the Hornet line. Of the four, the debonair Convertible Brougham was by far the most attractive model Hudson built in the 1950s. All four models were powered by a 308-cubic-inch in-line six-cylinder side valve engine, drawing fuel from a Carter two-barrel carburetor. The Twin-H option (twin carburetors) was added in 1952 and offered through 1954, as was a dual-range Hydra-Matic transmission in place of the standard column shift manual.

From 1951 through 1953, output from the L-head six with the single Carter was a substantial 145 horsepower at 3,800 rpm, 160 horsepower with the Twin-H.

In 1954, horsepower was raised to a vigorous 160 at 3,800 rpm and 170 horsepower with Twin-H. A nice way to go out. These were to be the last high-performance engines to emerge from Hudson as an independent automaker.

The new Hudsons featured an exclusive "step-down" chassis design that placed the passenger compartment within the frame members for all-around safety. This also allowed a lower overall height for the car—just 60³⁄₈ inches, a lower roofline without sacrificing headroom, and a lower center of gravity for better handling.

Proven in competition for three years, the entire Hornet line featured an A-arm and coil-spring independent front suspension and rugged solid-axle rear with semi-elliptical leaf springs. Further contributing to the Hornet's road-holding reputation were direct-acting shock absorbers at all four corners, a dual-acting front stabilizer, and a lateral stabilizer in the rear, combined with its low center of gravity and "Center-Point Steering" system. The Hudson was very likely the best-handling and best-built American car in its price class and a sure-fire contender for the 100 greatest cars of the twentieth century.

Isotta-Fraschini

8A SS Cabriolet

Were beauty alone the only reason for the Isotta-Fraschini's existence, it would have been reason enough. One would have to search long and hard to uncover an ungainly example of this proud marque, the true thoroughbred of Italian motorcars in its day.

It was in the dawning years of the automobile, before the turn of the century, that Cesare Isotta and the brothers Fraschini—Oreste, Vincenzo, and Antonio—formed a company to import Renaults into Italy. By 1902, they were producing their own automobiles using de Dion engines and Renault transmissions.

Societa Anomina Fabbrica di Automobili Isotta Fraschini, often referred to simply as IF, started producing its own engines in 1903 when Giuseppe Steffanini joined the firm as an engineering consultant. Their first all-Italian-built model, the Tipo 12 horsepower, launched three decades of Isotta-Fraschini engines and automobiles.

In the early 1900s, Isotta's marketing and sales priorities were directed not wholly toward Europe, as one would have expected, but far across the Atlantic to the eastern seaboard where race-prepared Isottas won the 1908 Briarcliff in New York, the Lowell Trophy in Massachusetts, and the Savannah Challenge Trophy race in Georgia. The strong showing by the Milanese firm resulted in their rapid climb in popularity among America's automotive elite.

Steffanini's work for IF—his last recorded design executed in 1914—was overshadowed by Giustino Cattaneo, who joined Isotta as technical director in 1905. For the next 30 years, virtually all that IF produced would be touched by Cattaneo—36 types of automobiles, 18 aero engines, and 19 types of industrial and military vehicles.

Following World War I, Isotta-Fraschini embarked upon its greatest era, with Oreste Fraschini directing the company's new postwar marketing and design strategies. The prewar years had seen a flurry of Isotta models and the firm's continued support and involvement in motorsports competition. The new Isotta policy would be to offer a single model, with an emphasis on luxury and elegance.

The new postwar car, the eight-cylinder Tipo 8, was introduced in August 1919. Until the war, IF had only built four-cylinder engines for their production cars. Cattaneo's new in-line eight was the first of its type put into series production anywhere in the world.

The Tipo 8 engine was a 90-horsepower overhead valve monobloc design, displacing 5,890 cc (359.4 cubic inches) with an 85 mm x 130 mm bore-and-stroke. A by-product of Cattaneo's aircraft engine designs, the Tipo 8 benefited from that technology by using a single casting aluminum block, steel-lined cylinders, and aluminum pistons.

Oreste Fraschini's new philosophy proved itself right, especially in America, where the Isotta continued to grow in popularity among the well-to-do.

Sadly, Oreste would not live to see the great Tipo 8 models that would come in the 1920s and 1930s: He died in 1921, and, not long after, his brothers and brother-in-law left the company, which was acquired by Count Lodovico Mazzotti. By the early 1920s, Isotta-Fraschini had established itself as one of the world's most desirable automobiles, and names on the firm's prestigious list of clients included the kings of Italy (Victor Emmanuel) and Iraq (Faisal), the Queen of Romania, the Empress of Abyssinia, Prince Louis of Monaco, the Maharajahs of Alwar and Patiala, and the Aga Kahn. In America, Clara Bow, Jack Dempsey, William Randolph

Hearst, and Rudolph Valentino had all become Isotta-Fraschini owners.

The Tipo 8 was followed by the 8A, 8AS (*Spinto,* or sports) version, which produced 135 horsepower, and the premium 8A SS (*Super Spinto*), delivering a stunning 160 horsepower and a factory-guaranteed top speed of 100 mph.

In America, where nearly a third of Isottas were sold, a chassis alone was priced at $9,750 in 1930, with coachbuilt upwards of $20,000.

The cars were treated to an investiture of coachwork by Europe's leading design studios. Carrozzeria Italiana Cesare Sala and Castagna were responsible for the majority of bodies built for the Tipo 8 series, with most of the balance accounted for by Stabilimenti Farina and Touring in Italy; Gurney Nutting, Hooper, and Lancefield in England; and Fleetwood in the United States.

Of the Italian coachbuilders all the Castagna brothers' designs for Isotta-Fraschini were the most dramatic. Nearly all were done by Emilio Castagna, who excelled in his selection of the finest (if not unique) materials. Interior appointments; fabrics; wood; cabinetry; and the subtle complementing of colors, shapes, and textures were Castagna trademarks.

In all, Tipo 8 production from 1919 to 1924 was 400 cars, Tipo 8A (S and SS) production from 1925 to 1931 numbered 950 cars, and just 20 examples of the Tipo 8B were built between 1931 and 1933, when the main factory in Via Monterosa began producing only aero engines. The Depression hit IF very hard, as its largest market was the United States. With virtually no automobile sales and only aircraft engines being built, IF was sold in 1933 to aircraft manufacturer Count Caproni di Taliedo, and both Mazzotti and Cattaneo took their leave.

Isotta-Fraschini attempted a return to automobile manufacturing after World War II, but the road that these great cars had once traveled no longer existed. The Isotta, like the classic era itself, had irrevocably become part of the past.

Jaguar
XK-120 Roadster

The assembly line moves painstakingly slowly at Jaguar's Browns Lane plant, a well-preserved structure quietly nestled amongst a line of patriarchal houses in the outskirts of Coventry, England. Here time is not so much of the essence as is craftsmanship. The assembly lines are slower than most, because Jaguars are built today with the same scrupulous attention to detail they were more than half a century ago.

Throughout the company's history, there have been only five major sports car models: the SS-100, XK-120, XKE, XJS, and XK-8. Each is dramatically different, yet all are cut from the same fabric—a multi-colored tapestry woven with threads of victory, innovation, elegance, and grace.

To most sports car enthusiasts, the Jaguar name is synonymous with postwar racing, particularly the C and D types' domination of LeMans in the early 1950s; however, Jaguar Cars and their SS predecessors had their humble beginnings back in 1931. Built to be both race cars and road cars, SS models were campaigned in various events throughout Great Britain and Europe in the 1930s, and it should be noted that William Lyons, founder of the firm, and later knighted for his efforts, did a fair amount of racing in his own right to prove the mettle of the motorcars he manufactured.

One of the greatest automotive minds of this century, Lyons began his career with the Crossley Car Company and, in 1922, established the original Swallow Side Car Company, or "SS Cars," moving to larger quarters in Coventry in 1928. In 1935, Lyons added the Jaguar name and mascot, and, after the war in Europe, he renamed the company Jaguar Cars Ltd., eliminating the initials *SS* which had picked up a profoundly distasteful connotation.

Coventry's first postwar models, though still outstanding in appearance, were based almost entirely on 1930s designs, as were just about every automaker's at the end of the war. In 1948, however, Lyons would create one of the most innovative and captivating automobiles of the twentieth century, the XK-120—a car so completely different that it would establish Lyons as a historic figure in his own lifetime.

The XK-120 was a totally modern automobile, not a revision of some shopworn prewar design. Seemingly overnight, it became one of the most sought-after sports cars in the world. From start to finish, Lyons took a mere three months to design the car and the factory a mere two weeks to ready a hand-built prototype for the 1948 Earls Court Motor Show.

The undercarriage for the XK-120 was derived from the Jaguar MK-V Saloon chassis, shortened some 18 inches and fitted with a new six-cylinder, twin-overhead camshaft engine, capable of producing 160 horsepower and a sustained top speed of 120 miles per hour—thus the *120* in the car's name.

The response at Earls Court was so overwhelming that Lyons immediately put the car into production, but it would take Coventry some 20 months to prepare tooling to build the bodies out of steel. In order to meet demands for the car, all XK-120s produced in 1949 and 1950 were made of aluminum, as had been the Earls Court prototype, making the early cars easily distinguishable.

For the late 1940s, the XK-120 was revolutionary in design. Lyons had not only started with a clean sheet of paper but a brand-new sketchbook, discarding anything that appeared to resemble prewar styling. The XK-120 featured a streamlined, ergonomic body different from any of its contemporaries. It was considerably wider than other sports cars, which allowed for larger and more comfortable leather seats. The curved exterior lines created large hollows inside the doors that were used for storage space, the openings tastefully covered with a leather flap. Instruments and

controls were housed in a leather-finished center fascia, affording the driver an undisturbed view of the gauges.

By design, the interior was intended to impart a higher level of comfort and decor than had previously been offered in European sports cars (with the exception of Alfa Romeos). Luggage capacity was another concern addressed by Lyons, and to that end he created a double-shelved trunk that allowed ample room for both the spare tire and a sizable portmanteau. With the top raised, additional storage space could also be found behind the seats.

Despite the air of luxury and comfort Lyons had provided, the XK-120 was not to be taken lightly in competition. It could accelerate from a stand to 60 mph in 10 seconds, and clock a quarter mile in 17 seconds flat. It handled with the best of its competitors and had, in fact, very few shortcomings. If one had to point out any

weakness in the Jaguar, it would have been the brakes, which had a tendency to fade under extreme use. History nevertheless remembers the car with few imperfections and many accolades. In America, the roadsters and coupés were embraced by sports-car cognoscenti and sports-car club racers alike.

In August 1949, drivers Leslie Johnson and Peter Walker finished first and second in a one-hour event at Silverstone behind the wheel of XK-120s. Johnson competed at Palm Beach Shores, Florida, in January 1950, finishing fourth in the car's first U.S. racing appearance. In the 1950 Mille Miglia, Johnson finished fifth overall. He also drove with a team of three factory XKs at LeMans and was up to second place when his clutch failed—and, mind you, this was essentially a production road car. In other events, rallyist Ian Appleyard won the 1950 Alpine. Stirling Moss won the Tourist Trophy race in Ireland, and an XK-120 was driven

Jaguar XKE Convertible

to victory at the first Pebble Beach races in 1950, by a then 23-year-old newcomer named Phil Hill.

This remarkable first full year of all-out Jaguar competition established the XK-120 as one of the greatest sports cars of its time, a car truly suited to both road and track. Jaguar, it seemed, could only go from strength to strength, and, in 1961, Sir William Lyons would prove that theory to be true with the introduction of one of the most famous sports cars of all time, the XKE.

The XK-120 and succeeding 140 and 150 models had established a new genre of sports car, and although Ferrari has since driven to the forefront of that métier, the cars Coventry put to road from 1948 through 1974 (the last year for the XKE) have left no less of an impression on the motoring world.

Though it has been almost four decades since the E-Type's debut in Geneva, the XKE is as contemporary in appearance as many of the latest European sports cars, including the Jaguar XK-8, which draws its styling influence from the original E-Type. Unlike so many other cars from the 1960s, the XKE has never grown old and is still fashionable nearly 40 years later.

In designing a successor to the XK-120, Lyons started once again with a clean sheet of paper, but one torn from the same pad. He had with one broad stroke reinvented the two-seat sports car. Defined within the context of the original 1948 XK-120, it was unhampered by the inelegant harmony of trim and 2 + 2 seating that affected the later XK-150 series. And like the XK-120 in 1948, the Jaguar XKE was about the fastest and most exotic-looking production sports car you could buy in 1961.

Though new from the ground up, the E-Type had its design and performance origins well rooted in the LeMans—winning Jaguar D-Types, and road-going XKSS model. The symmetry of line penned by Lyons and his design staff for the XKE was gleaned from the D-Type. In translating race car to road car, Lyons called upon themes that prospective buyers of the new Jaguar model and followers of Coventry's competition victories throughout the late 1950s might easily recognize—the large oval snout, the sweeping front and rear fender lines, and the prominent power bulge and hood louvers. For those who had owned and raced the production D-Types and later XKSS variants, the XKE was the closest anyone had come to building a roadworthy heir.

Not as quickly penned as the XK-120, it took Jaguar nearly four years to fully develop the XKE. The production cars, fixed-head coupé, and E-Type convertible, such as the handsome example pictured from the Thomas Reddington collection, benefited from the D-Jag's competition experience. Here was a true race-bred sports car, steeped in tradition, engineered to perform like no other production car on the road, and to do so with the driver in the surrounds of fine Connolly leather and handcrafted bodywork.

The E-Type measured 14 feet, 7$^{1/2}$ inches from end to end and 5 feet, 5$^{1/4}$ inches in width. The wheelbase stretch was 8 feet, and the track 4 feet, 2 inches. Setting off Dunlop RS5 6.40 tires were the E-Type's stunning 15-inch, 72-spoke wire wheels, the first use of 15-inch wheels on a Jaguar sports car. (As an option, purchasers could order the XKE fitted with Dunlop R5 racing tires, 6.00 front and 6.50 rear, mounted on painted competition wheels, the rear pair having rims half an inch wider.) The first cars were powered by the 3.8-liter six used previously in the later XK-150. Output

1967 JAGUAR XKE CONVERTIBLE

was the same, a substantial 265 horsepower and 206 ft lbs of torque.

In terms of handling, the E-Type was exemplary. One could pile on speed and enter a corner hell-bent without the fear of falling off a rapidly decreasing radius. The steering was neutral except at the limits where throttle-off oversteer could be induced, but with the convertible's low center of gravity, one could almost break the laws of physics before breaking loose the tires' grip on the road. For the average driver, and even the seasoned veteran—the E-Type was the best sports car money could buy, unless of course one had the financial means to purchase a Ferrari. Few did.

On both road and track, the 3.8-liter six had been the mainstay of Jaguar for years. In 1964, its displacement was increased to 4.2 liters and paired with an all-synchro-mesh gearbox. With easier operation, a slight (though not notable) increase in horse-power, and a sizable step up in torque, 240 ft lbs to 283 ft lbs, the 4.2 was quicker from a stand to 60, through the quarter mile, and up to 100 mph, than its predecessor. An improved clutch, a new exhaust system, and more comfortable seats seemed to cure

all of the E-Type's prior ills. It was, for the time, the consummate sports car.

E-Types raced and won many "touring car" events in England and Europe during the 1960s, driven by a host of well-known drivers, including Graham Hill, Bruce McLaren, and Roy Salvadori. Jaguar also built a number of lightweight, all-aluminum (including the engine block) Es, plus a "low-drag" coupé.

Although there was no direct competition on the showroom floor between Jaguar and Ferrari, the E-Type was in need of change after a decade of production. Thus with the new Series 3 V-12 introduced in 1971, the XKE was at once endowed with Ferrari-like imagery: power to reach 60 mph in 6.4 seconds, cover 1,320 feet in an average of 15 seconds, and drive the speedometer needle upwards of 135 mph. The V-12 engine was uncommonly quiet—the exhaust note leaving the four exhaust tips was deep and resonant. It was a lovely way to ring down the curtain on one of England's greatest sports cars.

The XKE was officially retired from the Jaguar line on February 24, 1975.

Kissel Speedster

The KisselKar lived its short but productive life from 1907 to 1931, a mere 24 years, during which time the Hartford, Wisconsin, company made what we call today state-of-the-art automobiles. Following World War I, "Kar" was dropped from the company name because it sounded too German. The Kissel family, however, like many others in Wisconsin, *was* German, having emigrated to the United States in the 1800s.

In 1905, two of Louis Kissel's sons, George and William, left the family business, which included the Kissel Manufacturing Company, the Hartford Plow Works, and the Hartford Electric Company, to build an experimental automobile. Their prototype was a four-cylinder runabout with shaft drive. Considering that the majority of automobiles in the world were utilizing chain drive, the Kissel brothers had taken a far more ambitious approach to transferring power from the engine to the wheels. A year later, they started producing KisselKar automobiles in Hartford.

The fledgling American automotive industry, especially companies in rural areas, used local talent to produce everything from frame and suspension components to bodies, which, for the early Kissels, were built by the Zimmermann Brothers, a firm previously noted for manufacturing sleighs in nearby Waupun, Wisconsin.

Around 1908, the Kissels hired a university-educated engineer named Herman Palmer and one J. Friedreich Werner, a German coachbuilder with impeccable credentials, including a stint with Opel Motor Works in Russelsheim. Within a year, the Kissel organization was offering a full line of automobiles, as well as a line of purpose-built truck chassis with capacities up to five tons. With few exceptions, the Kissels produced every component for their cars, including the engines.

KisselKars were always on the cutting edge of automotive design, which, in an era when every new idea was innovative, meant that the Wisconsin firm had to keep pace with Indiana and Michigan automakers such as American, Marmon, Cadillac, Packard, Oldsmobile, Buick, and Oakland. With Werner in charge of body design, however, Kissel coachwork was always in step with, if not slightly ahead of, the competition, as was Kissel's engineering.

In 1911, they introduced the double-drop frame (with a kickup over both front and rear wheels), and their use of three dash lamps under a steel cornice in 1914 pioneered indirect illumination of dashboard instruments. (Kissel was also one of the pioneers of roll-up windows.)

The majority of cars produced from 1915 on were powered by an L-head, six-cylinder engine of Kissel design, which remained in production, with only minor changes, until 1928. During the 1920s, Kissels were among the most stylish American cars on the road, particularly the "Gold Bug" speedster, which was introduced in 1919 and became a favorite among Hollywood film stars, who favored sporty, open roadsters. The cars were so popular, in fact, that the Los Angeles Kissel dealer was permitted to make specially equipped models with golf bags, removable fabric tops, and stylish Woodlite headlights.

The appearance of the sporty Kissels clearly set them apart from other open cars produced in the early 1920s and inspired many copies. The Gold Bug, however, was the original, and in traditional yellow colors, such as this example owned by William B. Ruger Sr., it is a truly stunning automobile worthy of its popularity. Ruger's 1923 Gold Bug is one of the few existing pre–classic era examples known to have been restored to authentic, original fit and finish.

In addition to its dashing coachwork—accented by a conspicuous absence of running boards; narrow, cut-down doors; and a beetleback decklid—the two-place speedster also featured unique outrigger seats that folded neatly into drawers on either side of the body. It was an idea that probably wouldn't get the approval of the National Highway Traffic Safety Administration today, but in the Roaring Twenties it was a jaunty way to take a couple of friends along for a ride!

Despite the Kissel's popularity, a mortgage for $750,000 had been taken out against property and machinery in 1921 in order to keep the doors open in a very competitive post–World War I market. Production of 2,123 cars in 1923 showed promise after the company had suffered through the postwar recession, but, in 1924, production tumbled back to a dismal 803 cars. The sudden drop in sales

meant little working capital, and Kissel's problems were compounded by retooling difficulties for the all-new 1925 model line, which would introduce Lockheed hydraulic brakes and a new Lycoming-based straight eight, utilizing Lycoming blocks fitted with Kissel aluminum heads. The delays pushed model introductions into the new year, forcing the company closer to financial collapse, despite an enthusiastic response to the new cars. Kissel closed the books on 1925 with an impressive 2,122 sales. The following year, however, purchases declined to 1,972, and that was the beginning of a backward slide that would culminate in 1929 with production dipping well below 1,000 cars, 200 of which were National-Kissel funeral cars distributed through the National Casket Company. This was a harbinger of hard times to come—by 1930, Kissel would be able to drive itself to its own

Lamborghini
350 GT

There was a time when Ferrari drivers used to look over their shoulders when a Maserati or Lamborghini approached, wondering whether or not they were going to be passed. Those were the days of the Miura and Ghibli and the 350 GT—a time when Italian sports cars were hell-bent for speed, and comfort and luxury were secondary considerations, if considerations at all. Today they are all fast, all luxurious, and, in a way, all the same, shaped by wind tunnels and designers schooled in the intricacies of aerodynamic form. Angels and ministers of grace defend us! Be thankful for times past when cars had distinctive lines, and a daring design meant raising the crown of the fenders higher than the hood.

Unlike Enzo Ferrari, Ferruccio Lamborghini wasn't building race cars in the early post–World War II years; he was busy building his fortune producing vechicles that ran a tad slower . . . by modifying surplus war vehicles into farm tractors. But Ferruccio also had a penchant for competition and spent part of his time tuning Fiat 500s and 1100s for road racing. He even drove a 500 Topolino in the 1948 Mille Miglia, which, incidentally, was won that year by a Ferrari.

In 1952 Lamborghini started building his own line of tractors and eventually became the third largest manufacturer in Italy, but it wasn't until 1963 that the then 47-year-old tractor builder decided to get into the manufacturing of high-performance sports cars. There are countless stories of exactly how Ferruccio Lamborghini got interested in the

business, but, in all likelihood, he had always wanted to build sports cars—it just took 20 years to amass the money to do it. But, of course, everyone prefers great fiction, and the best story is an argument between Enzo Ferrari and Lamborghini over a Ferrari Ferruccio had found fault with. The rough translation was something to the effect of "you go and build a car if you think you can do it better." This would have been accompanied by a significant number of hand gestures. Whatever, if anything at all, transpired at the 1963 Turin motor show, Ferruccio Lamborghini introduced the 350 GTV to the scribes of the motoring world, and they were not impressed.

The GTV was a bit confused: It had a body not too dissimilar from the later 350 GT but with somewhat awkward concealed headlights and a virtually useless center-mounted rear third seat. The design was turned over to the renowned firm of Touring in Milan, which swiftly reworked the front end and fenderlines into a sleek, sculptured body that even 34 years later still turns heads.

The cars were built in the patented Superleggera ("superlight") style developed by Touring in the 1930s. The bodywork was aluminum, affixed to a skeleton of steel tubes. The pop-up headlamps were ditched for Touring's stylish, wide, oval pods, which blended beautifully into the high-crowned fenders. The restyled model, now named the 350 GT, was introduced in March at the 1964 Geneva show, and this time to far better reviews.

Beneath the hood was the Lamborghini 60-degree

V-12 engine, designed by Giotto Bizzarrini and now fitted with six horizontal Weber carburetors (the prototypes had used vertical units), wet-sump lubrication, and a pair of Marelli distributors. The engine created 270 horsepower at 7,000 rpm through a five-speed all-synchromesh gearbox, and could reach a top speed of nearly 150 mph. Lamborghini knew where to do his shopping, and, for the transmission, he had deferred to the German firm of ZF, which supplied the five-speed used on both versions of the 350 GT.

With plenty of front and rear overhang on a short 100.4-inch wheelbase, low 48½-inch height, and wide 67-inch stance, with a track measuring 53.8 inches front and rear, the Touring body was very daring. The suspension was fully independent via coil springs and telescopic shock absorbers and equipped with four-wheel Girling disc brakes. Overall, the 350 GT was a more sophisticated design than a comparable 1964 Ferrari, giving some credibility to the story about Lamborghini finding fault with the design and quality of Ferraris. The V-12s from Modena had two overhead camshafts, Lamborghinis had four; they carried six carburetors instead of three and had a five-speed gearbox, bettering Ferrari's four-speed with overdrive.

In 1965, the year in which the example pictured from the Houston, Texas,

collection of Jerry J. Moore was built, Lamborghini increased the size of the V-12 to four-liters (by enlarging the bore from 77 mm to 86 mm), which added another 50 horsepower to the 350 GT, boosting output to an impressive 320 horsepower at 6,500 rpm, with a nine-to-one compression ratio.

The 350 GT was perhaps a better car than the comparable Ferrari in every way. *Car and Driver* noted in its March 1966 issue, "It is much less demanding to drive than a Ferrari, and what is more, it seems to steer, stop, go and corner just about as well as our Ferrari test car (275 GTS), but it is so smooth, and so quiet."

A mere 143 Lamborghini 350 GTs were built*, compared to 200 comparable Ferrari 275 GTS models of the period. Was Lamborghini the better of the two? Only history will tell. Today a Ferrari 275 GTS is worth considerably more. However, sometimes greatness is measured in more than monetary terms. No matter which model one prefers, there is no denying the significance of the 350 GT, the car that put Lamborghini's charging bull on the road.

---

*Lamborghini also produced one Zagato-bodied coupé and two or three Touring-bodied 350 GT convertibles. In 1966, the 400 GT 2 + 2 was introduced, adding two small rear seats, a somewhat modified rear-end design to accommodate the + 2 configuration, and the first use of quad headlights, an easily distinguished characteristic of the 400 GT 2 + 2.

Lamborghini Miura
P400

The Lamborghini Miura was as radical a departure from standard street machine practice as one could imagine, as was its introduction at the Turin car show in November 1965, where the P400 chassis was shown—with coachwork!

Nuccio Bertone (the story goes) was so impressed with the naked chassis that he proposed to drape it in proper garments to make a real car. Sr. Lamborghini accepted the offer, and the stunning result was completed in time for the Geneva show the following March.

The audience was so smitten by the audacity of the engineering and the beauty of the execution that the problem suddenly became how to get the car developed and built quickly enough to meet the demands of the world's rich playboys.

Rushed to market, early versions lacked some refinements expected by the café society buyers. The untinted windshield sloped back so far that the occupant sat in brilliant Italian sunshine. There was no air-conditioning, and the idea of a radio didn't arise, since the mechanical roar generated by chain-driven camshafts adjacent to one's head suggested earplugs. Other interesting details included a peculiar latch for the rear body section that didn't always latch. But the fundamentals were glorious—getting off the line was really startling, climbing modest hills in top gear was no trick at all, and the mechanical music never stopped.

Early road tests in enthusiasts' journals never included straight line maximum speed. There was reader suspicion

that the test drivers either (a) never found a paved space long enough, or (b) when they did, their daring turned to jelly.

As subsequent versions were brought to market, flaws were corrected, amenities appeared, and the Miura achieved a stature unchallenged—maybe even by its siblings.

The model pictured was originally owned by Dean Martin. Notes present owner Jay Leno, "The Miura car was sort of the catalyst for the era. It began an entire generation of rear-engined (amidships) designs from Italian automakers. It was never quite a finished car, so not everything was thought out. For example, you throw it into a left- or right-hand turn at speed and the oil pressure drops." Leno laughs and shakes his head in mock horror. "But they fixed that on the later models. There was also a tremendous amount of front-end lift at high speed, but it was a car built as much for styling as anything else; that's the way Bertone designer Marcello Gandini wanted it. This was probably the best-looking car Lamborghini ever built, but when the first Countach came along around 1973 everybody got excited and the Miura quickly faded from popularity.

"I like the Miura more than the Countach. I like a car where all four wheels are the same size, from the standpoint of how the car sits. The Miura has a definite sense of style, one man's idea of what a sports car should look like as opposed to wind tunnel tests and all that, which is probably a better way to do it, but you just don't see many sports cars like the Miura that were styled with no outside influences. It was made to look good, and that's that."

Lincoln KB
Dual Cowl Sport Phaeton

In 1932, when Ford equipped its new models with V-8 engines for the first time, the luxurious Lincoln division of Ford Motor Company introduced an all-new line of V-12 cars. This marked the beginning of the multicylinder wars of the 1930s, with Cadillac, Packard, Auburn, Pierce-Arrow, and Lincoln all offering twelve-cylinder engines, not to mention Cadillac's and Marmon's steel manifestations of American automotive might, the V-16. Thus, against the era's stiffest competition and flying in the face of the economic undertow cast from Wall Street, Lincoln weighed in with one of the most powerful engines of the 1930s, a massive 447.9-cubic-inch V-12 delivering a robust 150 horsepower, while tipping the scales at more than half a ton!

Lincoln divided its 1932 model line into the V-8–powered KA series, built on a 136-inch wheelbase chassis, and the V 12 KB series with a lengthy 145-inch stretch between the wheels. The following year, the KA would become a companion model to the KB, equipped with a smaller 381.7–cubic-inch displacement V-12 producing 125 horsepower, but it was the 1932 KB that would come to symbolize Lincoln's rank in the pantheon of classic American motorcars.

As Lincoln's new flagship, the KB was available in more than 25 different body styles, the most classic of which was the Murphy-bodied Dual Cowl Sport Phaeton, style number 232. The sporty four-passenger car was offered either with or without the rear cowl. For the KB, Lincoln utilized the dual-cowl design pioneered for Duesenberg by LeBaron, wherein a rear panel, with windshield spanning the width of the body, released when the doors were opened, allowing the entire cowl and windshield to tilt up and out of the way for passenger ingress or egress. Once seated, the passengers simply pulled downward on the cowl and it lowered and latched back into place. The rear windshield could either lie flat on the top of the cowl or

be erected along with large foldout wind wings, to provide passengers with the same isolation from the draft at speed as those seated in the front.

Because of the dual-cowl design, there was also a large span between the front and rear doors, allowing them to be hinged so that the driver's compartment doors opened conventionally, latched at the rear, while those in the back were hinged in reverse, or "suicide style," allowing them to latch from the front. This configuration was particularly advantageous for chauffeured cars, permitting the driver to quickly step out and open the rear door.

The Lincoln KB Dual Cowl Sport Phaeton, the sportiest open-body design ever produced for the formal KB chassis, was originally built by the Lincoln factory, but the majority were produced on order by the Walter M. Murphy Company in Pasadena, California, which had been providing custom coachwork to Edsel Ford's luxury-car division for several years. A very limited model, only 43 were built. This superb example from Otis Chandler's Vintage Museum of Transportation and Wildlife, chassis number KB676, is a consummate example of the magnificent classic-era Lincoln KB.

1932 Lincoln KB Dual Cowl Sport Pharton

Lincoln Judkins
V-12

Custom coachwork was nearing its end by the late 1930s, and many of the leading design houses of the era had already closed their doors by 1938. Judkins, in Merrimac, Massachusetts, was one of the last of the great American ateliers standing after the Great Depression, and, in 1938, lent vision to this luxurious two-door Coupe-Limousine, or Touring Coupé, built on the 136-inch-wheelbase Lincoln Model K chassis.

The inspiration for the oversized doors and unusual arched window treatment had come from French stylist Letourneur et Marchand, which had done a similar design in 1938 on the Delage D8 120 chassis. The flowing fastback roofline, executed by Judkins on this one-off custom, had been pioneered in 1933 by Pennsylvania coachbuilder Fleetwood for the Cadillac V-16 Aero Dynamic Coupe, shown at the Chicago Century of Progress Exposition. Thus the Judkins Lincoln was a true styling hybrid, quite unlike any other car of the late 1930s.

The sweeping pillarless body design was a true hardtop, supported only by the windshield and rakishly angled C-pillar sail panels. The Judkins' doors were so large that passengers could enter the rear compartment without having to tilt the front seatbacks forward.

A styling masterpiece, the car was driven by Mr. John B. Judkins himself, who nicknamed the design "Coupé de Voyage," in honor of its French influence. It was to be among the last cars bodied by the New England coachbuilder, who finally gave up the ghost in 1939 and closed down. In 1940, not only was Judkins gone, but so, too, was the mighty 12-cylinder Model K Lincoln.

This all-original unrestored example is now part of the Nethercutt Collection in Sylmar, California.

Lincoln Continental

A car that history can never forget, the 1940 Lincoln Zephyr Continental launched an automotive dynasty. Inspired by Edsel Ford, who had become the head of Ford Motor Company's luxury-car division following the acquisition of Lincoln from Henry M. and Wilfred C. Leland in 1922, the first Continental was designed for Edsel's personal use.

The body design by Edsel Ford and his chief stylist, Bob Gregorie, imitated the long hoods, sweeping front fenders, high, narrow grilles, and trim bumpers seen on sporty European road cars of the late 1930s.

With Lincoln as his personal sanctuary, the one place where he operated, for the most part, free of his father's opinions and control, Edsel Ford produced some of the finest motorcars of the early twentieth century. It was written that Edsel once said, "Dad makes the most cars in the world, now I will make the best."

In 1939, Edsel drove the first Continental around Boca Raton, Florida, where the Ford family had its winter estate. He was stopped so many times and received so many requests from wealthy friends for a car like his that Edsel decided to put the Continental into limited production the following year.

The first 50 cars delivered in 1940 were virtually hand-built in one corner of the Lincoln assembly plant using the V-12 Lincoln Zephyr as a foundation

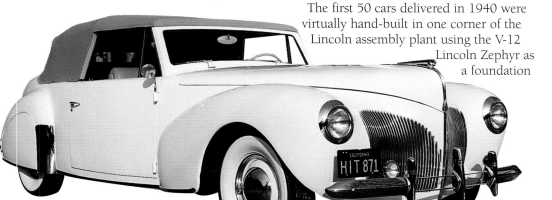

for the custom body. The very first Continental to be shipped to a dealer went to Long Beach, California, and was sold to film star Jackie Cooper. The sporty Cabriolet retailed for $2,840.

Originally cataloged as a special version of the Zephyr, the Continental became an individual Lincoln model line in 1941, with both Cabriolets and Club Coupes produced through 1942 and again after World War II until 1948. The first body design was revised in 1942, adopting most of the front-end sheet metal used on all the 1942 Lincolns, thus giving the cars a noticeably different appearance from the original design. Although still a very stylish car, the heavily chromed front visage somehow diminished the unique character of the 1940 and 1941 Continentals. Under the hood, the powerful Lincoln V-12 engine got a performance boost in 1942, being bored out to 305 cubic inches. Unfortunately, the cylinder walls were too thin, and, after a considerable number of engine failures, when production resumed after World War II the 1946 Lincolns were powered by the original 292-cubic-inch V-12 engine.

The Continental's return to production in 1946 was capped off with a Cabriolet model being chosen as the official pace car for the first postwar running of the Indianapolis 500 Memorial Day Classic. Edsel's son, Henry Ford II, was the pace car driver that year.

In the postwar era, front-end styling was revised from 1942 and made even busier-looking with a larger, double-tier grille. This imposing 1948 Coupe from the Nethercutt Collection was among the last of the original Continental to be produced. Discontinued in 1948, the Continental name would not return until 1956, with the introduction of the Continental Mk II.

Interestingly, the legendary name has nothing to do with the stylish rear-mounted spare. The name was chosen by Edsel Ford to reflect the car's European, or "continental," flair! However, every automobile that has since copied its styling from the Cadillac Sixty Specials to Ford's own 1956 and 1957 Thunderbirds, refers to the rear-mounted tire as a Continental spare.

Lincoln Continental
Mk II

The reprise of the Continental name came in 1956, with what was to become one of the most exclusive American cars of the decade, the Mk II. Lincoln heralded the new Continental's arrival as the "rebirth of a proud tradition." It was, in fact, much more, at least from a historical perspective.

The prestigious Continental name had been absent from the Lincoln line for eight years, but, moreover, so too had the handcrafted workmanship that made the original 1940 Continental an almost custom-built car. Mass production had become the order of business by 1956, with Detroit assembly lines turning out automobiles in record numbers, but, to manufacture the Continental Mk II, Ford returned to the old handcrafted ways.

The cars were almost entirely custom-built, according to exacting standards and material specifications, making the Continental Mk II the most expensive mass-produced American car ever offered for sale up to that time, with a staggering retail price of $9,966. Production was limited to just 2,550 cars in 1956 and a mere 444 the following year, plus two custom-built convertibles, one of which was for William Clay Ford, who was head of the Lincoln division.

The sleek four-passenger coupés had an overall height of just 56 inches, a length of 218.5 inches on a 126-inch wheelbase, and a width of 77.5 inches. The classic proportions of a long hood, short midsection, and rear deck—incorporating a modern interpretation of the original Continental spare—were penned by the team of John Reinhart, formerly chief of design for Packard, and legendary Auburn, Cord, and Duesenberg designer Gordon Buehrig. The distinctive styling of the Continental is considered by many to be the 1950s equivalent of Buehrig's hallmark

1936 Cord 810, another design that clearly stood head and shoulders above the competition.

Lincoln had at last outdone Cadillac, by creating a car so stunning in its appearance, so luxuriously appointed and calculatedly limited in production as to be without equal.

At the outset, Continental was organized as a new division of Ford Motor Company, with its own operations and an exclusive assembly plant in Ecorse Township, Michigan. The Mk II was built on a special chassis frame unlike any being used on production Lincolns. The powertrain, aside from a unique driveshaft arrangement, comprised Lincoln components that were hand picked. The engine was a 368-cubic-inch overhead-value V-8 specially tuned to deliver an estimated 285 horsepower, although the Continental division never officially disclosed the Mk II's horsepower—a Rolls-Royce marketing trait that Lincoln smartly appropriated.

Ford Motor Company had estimated that a break-even point of 2,500 units per year was necessary to make the Continental profitable, but, given the complexity of manufacturing the car, that number soon became unrealistic. In July 1956, the Continental division was incorporated into the Lincoln division as a cost-saving measure.

The Mk II was only produced for two years; however, there is no actual 1956 or 1957 model year designation. The Continental was considered a model series, although cars built between June 1955 and September 1956 were registered as 1956 models, and those built thereafter were technically considered 1957s. The Mk II breathed new life into Edsel Ford's legendary Continental, which to this very day remains Lincoln's premier model.

Marmon Wasp Speedster

Every automaker has its moment of glory. For some, it's at the beginning of their history, for others it's in the middle, and, for a few, it comes at the end. For Indianapolis, Indiana, manufacturer Nordyke and Marmon, one of the most distinguished American makes of the early twentieth century, it was all of the above.

Howard Marmon was chief engineer of his family's milling machinery business, Nordyke and Marmon, and in 1902 he completed his first prototype automobile. Although strictly experimental, it was remarkably progressive for its time, featuring an overhead-valve air-cooled two-cylinder engine in 90-degree V configuration, a multiple-disc clutch in the flywheel, a three-speed selective sliding-gear transmission, a subframe carrying engine and transmission with single three-point suspension, a force-fed lubrication system, and a shaft drive. Most of these features were years ahead of their time, and nearly all were utilized in Marmon's first production automobile, which arrived in 1904.

Having a foundry at his disposal, Marmon was able to design and manufacture special components for his cars, and soon the entire body was made of aluminum, as well as much of the running gear. In 1909, Marmon changed to a conventional in-line four-cylinder, water-cooled engine, and, from that time on, all Marmons used water cooling and conventional in-line T-head engines.

The most significant Marmon of the early 1900s was the Model 34, introduced in 1916 and followed by the Model 34B in 1920, the car acclaimed by many as Marmon's greatest product.

The Marmon 34 design incorporated the running boards, their supporting members, and the splash pans into the load-bearing structure. Although the bare chassis was somewhat unusual in appearance, it proved to be a breakthrough in platform design, achieving both a reduction in weight and an increase in strength. The advanced design of the Model 34 series featured "unification construction," making the body and chassis nearly one—essentially an early version of unibody construction, which would not become an industry standard for decades. Regarded as one of the best-handling cars on the road in 1916, the Model 34 had an even 50–50 front-to-rear weight distribution.

Marmon offered a variety of body styles. The bodies for the very popular Model 34B Speedsters were manufactured by the Hume Body Company of Rochester, New York, and made entirely of lightweight aluminum over a braced framework of ash. Total weight of the Speedster was a mere 3,295 pounds.

The Marmon 34B Speedster was noted for its distinc-

1920 MARMON WASP SPEEDSTER

tive appearance and exceptional speed—quick enough, in fact, to have indeed been a race car. Fitted with a special 3.0:1–ratio axle, a Speedster was timed around the 2½-mile Indianapolis Motor Speedway at two minutes, six seconds—an average of 71 miles per hour—an exceptional top speed for anything in 1920 that wasn't there to race. That same year, the Speedster was chosen as the Official Pacesetter for the eighth running of the Memorial Day classic, with Barney Oldfield as the driver.

To everyone's amazement, Oldfield led the starting grid around Indy at a sensational 80-mph clip before pulling off at the end of the pace lap. Even Oldfield's legendary rival, Ralph DePalma—who was on the pole that year—remarked that the Marmon may have been the fastest car on the track. Oldfield was so impressed with the Speedster's performance that he purchased the car after the race. Oldfield then

drove the Marmon coast-to-coast eight times to promote a line of tires bearing his name.

Oldfield's cross-country trips made the Speedster so popular with the public that on August 20, 1920, Marmon announced production of a Wasp Speedster in Marmon Racing Yellow, equipped with the special 3.0:1 axle (3.75:1 was standard) and a 0–100 mph speedometer. Identical to the Indy Pacesetter, with matching wire wheels, Goodrich or Goodyear cord tires, black radiator shell, fenders, dust deflectors, running gear, and nickel-plated metal trim, these 1921 models may well represent the first actual instance of a manufacturer offering replicas of an Indianapolis 500 Pace Car.

The Model 34B pictured, owned today by collector Jack Dunning, is the actual Marmon Wasp Speedster owned by the legendary Barney Oldfield in 1920.

Maybach Zeppelin

The automobile, both here and abroad, has become one of modern man's pre-eminent obsessions, one of the few objects that we assume to be extensions of our own personality. Like a bespoke suit or a lavish home, an automobile makes a statement about its owner. In the early years of the automotive trade, it also made a statement about its builder. The cars of Wilhelm and Karl Maybach spoke volumes about their creators.

Wilhelm Maybach was Gottlieb Daimler's friend and protégé throughout the early years of Daimler Motoren Gesellschaft and was instrumental in developing the ground-breaking 1901 Mercedes, but Maybach's role at DMG would change after Gottlieb Daimler's death in March 1900 at the age of 66.

Maybach found himself in disfavor with the DMG board, which consigned him, along with his son Karl, a brilliant engineer in his own right, to head of research and development, a far less important role than Maybach's earlier position as technical director under Gottlieb Daimler. It was, in the end, a political strategy to strengthen the position of Daimler's two sons, Paul and Adolf, but at the cost of Maybach's prestige within the company. In October 1906, Maybach decided to resign and officially left DMG in April 1907. He was 61 years old.

Rather than retire, he joined Count von Zeppelin in the development of a new aero engine for his giant air ships. Both Maybach and his son worked on the Zeppelins and, after World War I, branched out into the manufacturing of automobiles. The first, the Model W 3, was introduced in 1921, powered by a Maybach 70-horsepower straight six and two-speed transmission.

The new automobiles were actually the work of Karl, but, in the background, the father and teacher, Wilhelm, was always present. Although Mercedes were regarded as very stylish automobiles, the majority of Maybach body designs were conservative in nature, like the company's humble Swabian founder. The six-cylinder models were primarily bodied as limousines, pullman-cabriolets, sports cabriolets, and four-door cabrio-

1932 MAYBACH ZEPPELIN

lets, most of which were built by Karosserie Hermann Spohn in Ravensburg. The cars were competitive with those built by Mercedes-Benz, and, in 1929, the same year that the Graf Zeppelin circled the world, Maybach introduced the company's first V-12 automobile, a car intended to outclass the finest Mercedes-Benz models and compete against such lofty makes as Rolls-Royce and Hispano-Suiza.

The 12-cylinder DS marked the high point of Maybach's career. Sadly, it was his last accomplishment. Wilhelm Maybach passed away on December 29 at age 83, but not before his son had paid him tribute by building a car that even Daimler-Benz could not offer.

Karl Maybach followed the 1929 12 with the 150-horsepower seven-liter V-12

DS 7 model in 1930. That same year, the Maybach 12 was renamed the Zeppelin in honor of the historic global flight. In 1931, an even more powerful eight-liter version was introduced. The DS 8 series was manufactured though 1940. The Maybach Zeppelins came to be regarded as one of Germany's leading high-status luxury cars. Very limited in number, only around 300 were produced, over a period of 10 years.

The example pictured, from the Nethercutt Collection, was built in 1932 and bodied by Karosserie Spohn in Ravensburg as a four-door cabriolet. Delivering 200 horsepower, the Maybach V-12 displaced 7,977 cc, 485.3 cubic inches, or eight liters, depending on your favorite nomenclature. Despite the size and weight of the car, better than three tons, the luxurious Zeppelin cabriolet could reach a top speed of 100 miles per hour.

MG TC

1952 MG TD
1954 MG TF

They were uncomfortable, seldom ran properly, and were totally impractical. You had to love them.

There was, and still is, an inexplicable allure to the little Morris Garages, Ltd., (MG) cars built in Abingdon-on-Thames, Oxfordshire. In a way, they were the catalyst for countless other European sports cars and certainly the reason Chevrolet decided to experiment with a sports car of its own in 1953, namely the Corvette. But long before G.I.'s were coming home from "over there" with used MG TBs and a handful of new MG TCs in tow, the British automaker had been building sporting two-seaters, sedans, tourers, and, yes, even race cars.

It began in 1922, when an engineer named Cecil Kimber was hired on at Morris Garages as general manager. Tired of the uninspired Morris Cowley and Oxford saloons the company was building, Kimber began experimenting with two- and four-seat sports models built from off-the-shelf parts. To everyone's surprise, with the possible exception of Kimber himself, the sports models became eminently more popular than the standard Morris fare, and commanding a price nearly one-third more than the saloons.

Recognizing a good idea, Morris organized the MG Car Company, Ltd., on July 21, 1930, and appointed Kimber managing director with the responsibility for both design and production. Kimber's management and decisiveness was indisputable, and the MG staff obediently followed his dictum throughout the 1930s, by which time the little car with the double-hump cowl, cutaway doors, and slab-mounted rear fuel tanks had become one of England's most popular marques, and championed British prestige in motorsports when other seemingly more illustrious makes had eaten the dust of foreign competitors. From 1933 to 1935, MGs scored countless victories, including the 1933 Ulster Tourist Trophy and the team prize in the 1933 Mille Miglia! Although MG officially withdrew from competition in 1935, cars in the hands of privateer racers continued the MG's cannonade across Europe up until the beginning of World War II.

By 1939 the MG P-Type Midget, MG TA, and MG TB roadsters had established the marque, and no matter what type of car the men of Abingdon built, including some rather handsome four-passenger sedans and cabriolets, whenever the MG name was mentioned, the first image that came to mind was one of Kimber's sporty two-seaters.

With the onset of World War II, MG turned to the manufacture of aircraft, tanks, and amphibious vehicles. Cecil Kimber, still at work on a new MG model to be introduced when the war ended, never saw his dream realized. He died in a London railway accident in February 1945.

When the postwar dust cleared, MG went back into production with the basic prewar design. The only thing that had been wrong with the 1939 MG TB had been its width—the car was too narrow. Thus the first postwar MG, the TC, was made four inches wider, a tad sleeker, and powered by a 1250-cc four-cylinder engine developing an adequate 54.4 horsepower. With its beautifully balanced four-speed gearbox and 5.13:1 rear-axle ratio, the TC had a dashing sort of performance, quick off the mark and through the gears. It was not overly fast, with a top end just over 65 mph, but when you got down to it, speed wasn't everything—it was the feeling

you got sitting behind the wheel; the rush of air over the windshield; the feel of the road only inches below the seat cushion; and the handsome look of the MG's flowing fenders; the upright, foursquare radiator; and the big 19-inch wire-spoke wheels. The MG had character—white, starched, British character—and just enough charm to excuse all its shortcomings.

The TD took the postwar design just a bit further in 1950 and opened the door to an entirely new market, the United States. By 1952 there were 7,449 MGs registered and the MG had become the most popular imported sports car in the country, giving American automakers a new vision of the future.

The TD was replaced by the more modern TF version in 1954, and, in 1955, MG introduced the all-new MGA, its first modern sports car, bringing an end to more than 20 years of MG T series production.

1948 MG TC • 1952 MG TD • 1954 MG TF

MGA Twin Cam

MG was the answer.

The question really wasn't important. If it involved sports car club racing in the late 1940s and early 1950s, the answer was almost always MG, the most affordable two-seater one could buy. It was, however, dated and outclassed, if not in engineering and suspension, then certainly in appearance, with styling that had its roots firmly planted in the late 1930s.

In 1955, the British automaker finally made a total break from the original MG design, abandoning the old prewar styling in favor of a sleek envelope body that would give MG instant parity with the likes of Austin Healey, Triumph, Jaguar, and Porsche.

The design of the MGA body had an almost timeless simplicity, with smooth, flowing lines, high arched fenders, and a deliberate absence of chrome trim, extending even to the lack of door and trunk lid handles. The aerodynamic efficiency of the design easily proved its worth, returning an average increase in top speed of 15 mph over the old square-rigged models with no increase in horsepower.

The MGA suspension utilized an independent front with coil springs and unequal length wishbones and, at the rear, a traditional solid axle with semi-elliptical leaf springs.

One year after MG introduced the MGA roadster, a coupé version was shown at the 1956 London Motor Show. It would be the first factory-built coupé in more than 20 years and would closely resemble the roadster, with its optional removable hardtop in place. The coupé further improved aerodynamics enough to push the MGA over the 100-mph barrier in stock form, but club racers still wanted more. MG gave it to them . . . eventually.

In March 1953, MG started work on a Twin Cam version, which was originally intended for a very select market of amateur racers. The production goal was to be only

1960 MGA TWIN CAM

25 cars a week, and the company stated that it wanted to "steer them around to those enthusiast people who would know how to handle them throughout the world." As it turned out, steering them around MG was problem enough. The Twin Cam project would ultimately take five years to develop, and the new models would not be formally introduced until July 1958.

The Twin Cam was basically an improved MGA that, according to the gear ratios used, could go some 20 miles per hour faster and do it considerably quicker than a stock MGA, especially in the driving ranges between 40 and 100 miles per hour. Having made a car that much quicker, MG built in an equal opposite, fitting the Twin Cam models with Dunlop disc brakes on all four wheels.

Two specific items combined to give the Twin Cam its speed. First, the basic MG B-type block was punched out to a new bore size of 2.969 inches (up from 2.87) for a total displacement of 1,588 cc, or 96.906 cubic inches. Second, the double overhead cam alloy head gave the engine an additional 1,500 rpm at the top end. Where the standard pushrod MGA motors began to taper off, the Twin Cam was just starting to belt out its newfound puissance, with the horsepower rating shooting up from 76 to 98 in the space between 4,000 and 5,000 rpm. At the limit, output was 108 horsepower at 6,700 rpm.

What was it like to drive the Twin Cam? It was, in the American jargon of the late 1950s and early 1960s, "an E-ticket ride." Through the gears, the Twin Cam quickly drove the tach needle toward 7,000 rpm, and the additional 20-plus horsepower pressed driver and passenger firmly back into their seats. Handling was virtually the same as with a regular MGA, which is to say, very good. As owners have noted, though, the engine was always quirky, and MG continually worked on refining it until production ended. They never quite succeeded.

As a J production racer, the Twin Cam was a successful car, bringing countless victories to MG in the hands of privateer racers the world over. As a street car, it was a handful for most owners, far more difficult to manage than the MGA 1500 and later Mark II 1600s.

The MGA in all its variations had become the most popular sports car ever built by the time it went out of production in June 1962. Over seven years, MG sold more than 100,000 MGAs, including 2,111 Twin Cam models manufactured from September 1958 through June 1960.

For MG, the Twin Cam, such as this superbly restored example owned by Frans Nelson, would represent Abingdon's high-water mark for performance and styling. Sadly, it would also become one of MG's most troublesome cars. Too good for most drivers—difficult to maintain and easily prone to engine problems—as a limited production club racer it was nearly perfect, and in the end, that was all that really mattered.

Benz
Patent-Motorwagen

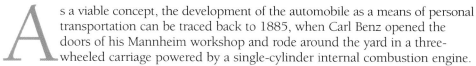

As a viable concept, the development of the automobile as a means of personal transportation can be traced back to 1885, when Carl Benz opened the doors of his Mannheim workshop and rode around the yard in a three-wheeled carriage powered by a single-cylinder internal combustion engine. The gasoline engine was not a new idea in the 1880s. Large, stationary engines had been in use since the latter part of the nineteenth century to power industrial and farming machinery. In fact, both Daimler and Benz had pioneered the development of stationary engines. It was the advent of a small single-cylinder motor that provided the one cohesive element allowing the inventions of many—Carl Benz included—to become a phenomenon—the automobile.

The first successful model of its kind, the 1886 Benz Patent-Motorwagen was powered by a water-cooled single-cylinder horizontal engine. The piston and cylinder were oriented fore and aft, and displacement was 954 cc, or 58 cubic inches. Output was a mere 0.75 horsepower at 400 rpm but sufficient to propel the three-wheeler at speeds of up to 10 miles per hour. The exposed connecting rod and crankshaft drove an attractively sculpted flywheel beneath the engine. From there, power went via a leather belt to a rudimentary differential and thence to both wheels by chain drive. The driver started the engine by spinning the flywheel by hand. Ignition was by coil and battery, and Benz had to invent his own spark plug.

On January 29, 1886, Carl Benz was granted German patent number 37435 for his invention—the Benz Patent-Motorwagen—recognized today as the first automobile and the source of all that has followed for more than a century.

1886 BENZ PATENT-MOTORWAGEN

Mercedes

The 1900s marked the beginning of an era when enterprise and progress in the development of personal transportation literally advanced by leaps and bounds from mere single-cylinder motor-driven carriages to automobiles capable of carrying passengers at 60 mph, a speed once thought to be beyond human endurance.

Almost a century ago, in 1901, the modern motorcar was born in Cannstatt, Germany. The car was the Mercedes, built by one of Europe's first successful automakers, Daimler Motoren Gesellschaft, what is today DaimlerChrysler AG. The 1901 Mercedes, named after Mercedes Jellinek, the daughter of the company's largest investor, Emil Jellinek, made every other motorcar built up to that time obsolete in a single day.

Sadly, Gottlieb Daimler never lived to see the first Mercedes. He succumbed to a worsening heart condition in March 1900, leaving the company, which he had founded in 1890, to the DMG board of directors, his son Paul, and Daimler's longtime friend and chief engineer, Wilhelm Maybach. The benchmark design for the '01 Mercedes, which gave rise to a new era in motorcar manufacturing, was already under development by Mayback and Paul Daimler in 1900, essentially the kind of car Jellinek had been beseeching his fellow Daimler Motoren Gesellschaft board members to manufacture since 1897. The wealthy Austro-Hungarian sportsman finally convinced DMG to proceed with production by agreeing to buy the first cars himself. He had only one stipulation: that the new automobile be named after his daughter.

As Jellinek had foreseen, the 1901 Mercedes became an immediate success, and production demands soon outstripped the capabilities of the

Cannstatt headquarters. Thus, around 1904, production was moved to a larger facility in the Untertürkheim district of Stuttgart.

The 1902 Mercedes pictured, a typical open body style of the era, is arguably the oldest existing Mercedes motorcar in the world, one of only 35 built by Daimler Motoren Gesellschaft at the original Cannstatt factory in 1902. Production continued in Cannstatt until the building was razed by fire on June 10, 1903, and everything, including all of the serial numbers and factory records from 1901 on, were lost, which is why we say that this is *arguably* "the oldest Mercedes." There is a second '02 in existence in England, and no one knows for certain which is actually older.

In the overall scheme of things, this car should not be judged simply on the merit of its being the oldest in the world but on the simple fact that the 1902 Mercedes was one of those rare designs where everything worked right.

It can be said that, until the introduction of the Mercedes, the motorcar had yet to emerge from the horseless carriage era. Jellinek, Maybach, and the Daimler *werke* quite literally pioneered the basic concept of the modern-day automobile. The '01

and '02 models introduced many innovations, including the honeycomb radiator and four-speed transmission, and for the era, the Mercedes' 40-horsepower Daimler engine was one of the most powerful in the world.

Until the advent of the Type 28/95 six-cylinder ohc models in 1914, the '01 and '02 designs were the foundation for every Mercedes motorcar built, including the factory competition cars that were victorious in hundreds of races for more than a decade.

As a new century begins in 2001, the modern automobile, the Mercedes, will celebrate its first centenary, and this 1902 model will be the car around which the laurels will be laid.

Mercedes

Labourdette Skiff

I n the early 1900s, Mercedes styling ran the gamut from conservative formal limousines and landaulettes to dashing phaetons and high-spirited sport two-seaters. None, however, approached the styling of the one-off 1911 Labourdette Skiff, the most exotic nonracing Mercedes built prior to World War I.

The Avenue des Champs-Elysées atelier of Henri Labourdette pioneered the exquisite wooden skiff torpedo design in 1910, a body style that would become eminently popular in Europe during the 1910s and remain so well into the early 1920s.

For Labourdette, wood seemed the most appropriate medium in which to work, because his skiff design was a boatlike body attached to an automobile chassis. The luster of varnished wood, its color, depth, textures, and grain, appealed to Labourdette in a way mere metal could never match. Certainly steel was the foundation upon which the automobile was built and, in most cases, bodied, but the Labourdette skiff was more: It was a benchmark in the history of early coachbuilding.

The triple-layer body was created by crisscrossing tiers of mahogany over a ribbed frame, then applying a third horizontal layer atop the substructure. To preserve the rigidity, doors were kept as small as possible in number and size. Apart from its attractiveness, a skiff body was light, normally weighing about 400 pounds. This was partly because the varnished wooden framework was left visible, eliminating the need for interior panels and trim.

We might marvel at these cars today and wonder how a single body could have justified so much work—the hundreds of individual hand-cut strips of mahogany and thousands of copper nails used to attach the planks to the body's hand-built wooden framework. In 1911, people were no doubt equally compelled to express wonderment when this 37/90 horsepower Mercedes chassis was fitted with a skiff body—the only known example of a Labourdette skiff ever mounted to Mercedes running gear.

Produced from 1910 through 1914, the 37/90 was powered by a four-cylinder engine with a bore and stroke of 130 mm x 180 mm (5 x 7 inches), displacing 9530 cc (approximately 400 cubic inches), and delivering 90 horsepower at 1,300 rpm. The in-line engine had two blocks of two cylinders each, with three overhead valves per cylinder, and a single camshaft mounted high in the crankcase. Fuel delivery was through a single Mercedes sliding-piston carburetor. A four-speed gearbox, with a gate change shifter mounted outside the body, delivered the engine's puissance to a chain-driven rear axle. Daimler Motoren Gesellschaft estimated the average top speed for the cars at 115 km/h—roughly 70 mph—although it was reported that with lightweight coachwork they could reach almost 100 mph.

At this point in DMG history, 1908 to 1912, there were two schools of thought on driving the rear wheels of an automobile. One was the innovative, although not altogether novel, shaft drive concept designed by Paul Daimler in 1907, wherein a propeller shaft connected to the transmission at the back of the engine delivered power to a rear differential, thence to the wheels. The other involved the logical, tried and true, gear-driven chain drive. It had worked on bicycles long before the motorcar existed, and on early motorized cycles (Gottlieb Daimler designed one in 1885); consequently the idea served its maker well in turning the rear wheels of the first Mercedes in 1901.

Chain drive had long proven to be the most durable, albeit not always the most reliable, means of driving the rear wheels. The heavy chains slipped and required adjustment, gear teeth broke, lubrication was a constant concern, and the noise at speed was thunderous. But chain drive worked, and it worked on everything from rudimentary voiturettes to race cars, including the 200-horsepower 1913 Mercedes Rennsportwagen and Sport-Phaetons. Chain drive was a natural, then, for one of the most powerful standard production models Mercedes offered, the 37/90.

Power was dispensed via a cone clutch and short driveshaft to a transaxle powering fully enclosed dual-inch and one-quarter pitch chains. The chain-drive enclosures, which were stylishly contoured and embellished with silver star emblems on the housing, kept the chains lubricated in an inch and a half of heavy oil and prevented dirt and grease splatter from being flung upon the body of the car, as had been the case in the past

with exposed chain drives. The jack shaft (rear axle), which delivered power to the chains, incorporated in-board mechanical brakes that provided almost twice the stopping capability as traditional wheel-mounted brakes, and offered the added advantage of lowering the car's unsprung weight.

According to research conducted by current owner B. Scott Isquick, the 37/90 horsepower chassis for the skiff was delivered to the Labourdette atelier at 35 Avenue des Champs-Elysées, Paris, in 1911 on behalf of the car's owner, American hatmaker Henry G. Stetson. The completed skiff was delivered to Stetson's Elkins Park residence outside Philadelphia in 1912 through the Mercedes dealer in New York City. The car cost Stetson an incredible $18,000!

The Labourdette body was removed from the chassis in 1922 after it was damaged in an accident, and a new Cape Top body was built by Camden Coachworks in New Jersey. Presumably, the original Skiff body was destroyed. Isquick first saw the car in the late 1960s, and, in 1972, he purchased it from Stetson. "Not directly, mind you," says Isquick. "Stetson had moved from Pennsylvania to Tucson, Arizona, by then, where he had a spread called the Rancho Sombrero, but we spoke." He recalls, "The Mercedes was quite well known in Philadelphia, having been driven around the Fairmount Park race course back in the 1910s by the legendary Ralph DePalma. Henry Strong, who was the president of the Stetson Manufacturing Company, had pictures of the car showing the Labourdette body, and that was the first time I saw the Mercedes as it was originally built."

After purchasing the car, Isquick decided to have the skiff rebuilt rather than restore the Camden body. Following Labourdette's original design specifications, the framework was recreated in ash, with steam-bent vertical spars used to support the mahogany planking and hickory trim. Following the labor-intensive process used by Labourdette more than 80 years ago, it required 2,700 brass rivets to attach the exterior wood to the ash frame! The entire project took restorer Dale Adams of Kent, Ohio, two years and 12,600 hours to complete!

Today the restored Labourdette Skiff has joined the ranks of the world's rarest and most significant automotive designs and has become so popular that in 1998 the Franklin Mint produced a scale model of the car.

Mercedes-Benz
Model K

Either by destiny or by chance, war has played a pivotal role in the history of Daimler and Benz. The War to End All Wars left Germany's economy on perilous ground after the 1918 armistice, and, by the early 1920s, there were precious few buyers for new and expensive automobiles in Europe, and Germany in particular, where only one German in 280 had the money to afford a car.

By 1924, the German automotive industry was moribund. In addition to Benz and Daimler, there was Horch, Opel, Auto Union, Wanderer, and Adler, to name but a few. In all, there were 86 German companies building a total of 144 different models. With such competition, Benz and Daimler found themselves forced closer and closer together, and, on May 1, 1924, the two firms entered into an agreement of mutual interest, a noncompetitive and cooperative arrangement that served as a prelude to their merger in June 1926. This marriage of necessity consolidated their engineering and production capabilities into the largest automobile manufacturing company in Germany.

Though each was successful individually, when Benz und Cie. and Daimler-Motoren Gesellschaft became Daimler-Benz AG, they became a force to be reckoned with. The first product of their combined effort, aside from the little-changed, traditional, lower-priced Mannheim and Stuttgart models, was the Model K, introduced in 1926.

The majestic K was more of an evolutionary design than a completely new luxury automobile. Based upon the Type 630 Mercedes 24/100/140 PS introduced in 1924, it was principally the work of the company's new chief engineer, Professor Ferdinand Porsche, and that of his predecessor, Paul Daimler, who had departed in 1922 for Horch.

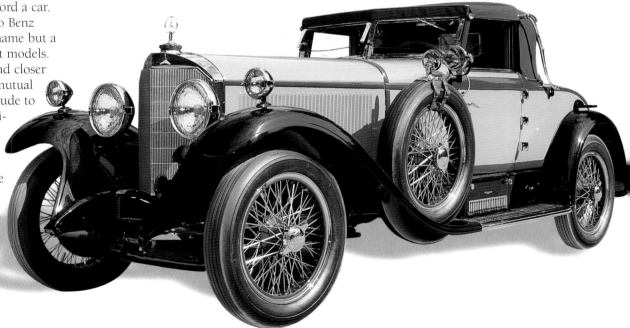

1927 MERCEDES-BENZ MODEL K

Professor Porsche improved upon Daimler's pioneer overhead camshaft six-cylinder engine design, which utilized a Roots-type supercharger to endow the massive K models with unparalleled straight-line performance. In 1926 the Model K became the fastest standard model of its type in the world, capable of a top speed in excess of 90 mph.

As to the K's road manners, any change over the previous Model 630, however minor, would have been considered an improvement. The 630's stiff underpinnings, semi-elliptic leaf springs at all four corners, and cumbersome channel-section chassis had imparted anything but a luxurious ride. The K introduced an improved suspension design on a shorter wheelbase, 134 inches versus the 630's 147.5 inches; thus the "K" designation in this instance stood for *Kurz* ("short" in German), rather than for *Kompressor*, as on later supercharged models like the SSK.

Along with less overall weight and a more responsive suspension, Professor Porsche also increased the output of the supercharged six-cylinder engine, which previously had created 100 horsepower without the supercharger engaged and 140 horsepower when the driver floored the accelerator pedal to turn on the blower. The revised Porsche engine delivered 110 and 160 horsepower, respectively. Porsche achieved this through a higher compression ratio (5.0:1, up from 4.7:1) and better ignition by using two spark plugs per cylinder. With a bore and stroke of 94 mm x 150 mm (3–11/16 x 5–29/32 inches), the Model K displaced 6.24 liters, or approximately 381 cubic inches. The 630's four-speed gearbox, with straight-cut gears, a challenge to downshift even for experienced drivers, was one of the few mechanical carryovers from the earlier model.

The example pictured, a 1927 sport cabriolet, was fitted with a body built in France by two Americans, Thomas Hibbard and Howard "Dutch" Darrin, who established Hibbard & Darrin of Paris in the 1920s. Two of the original partners in LeBaron Carrossier in New York, Hibbard and Darrin went to Paris to set up a European division of LeBaron and instead decided to go into business for themselves. Hibbard & Darrin were responsible for some of the finest and most advanced coachwork to come out of France throughout the 1920s and early 1930s.

Designing coachwork for the Model K chassis, the talented team created a number of body designs, including a four-door cabriolet, the Imperial limousine, and several two-passenger body styles similar to this sporty two-tone blue cabriolet.

As a transitional car during the Mercedes and Benz consolidation, the Model K proved to be an excellent bridge, regardless of the coachbuilder or body style, and a true benchmark in the history of Germany's greatest automaker.

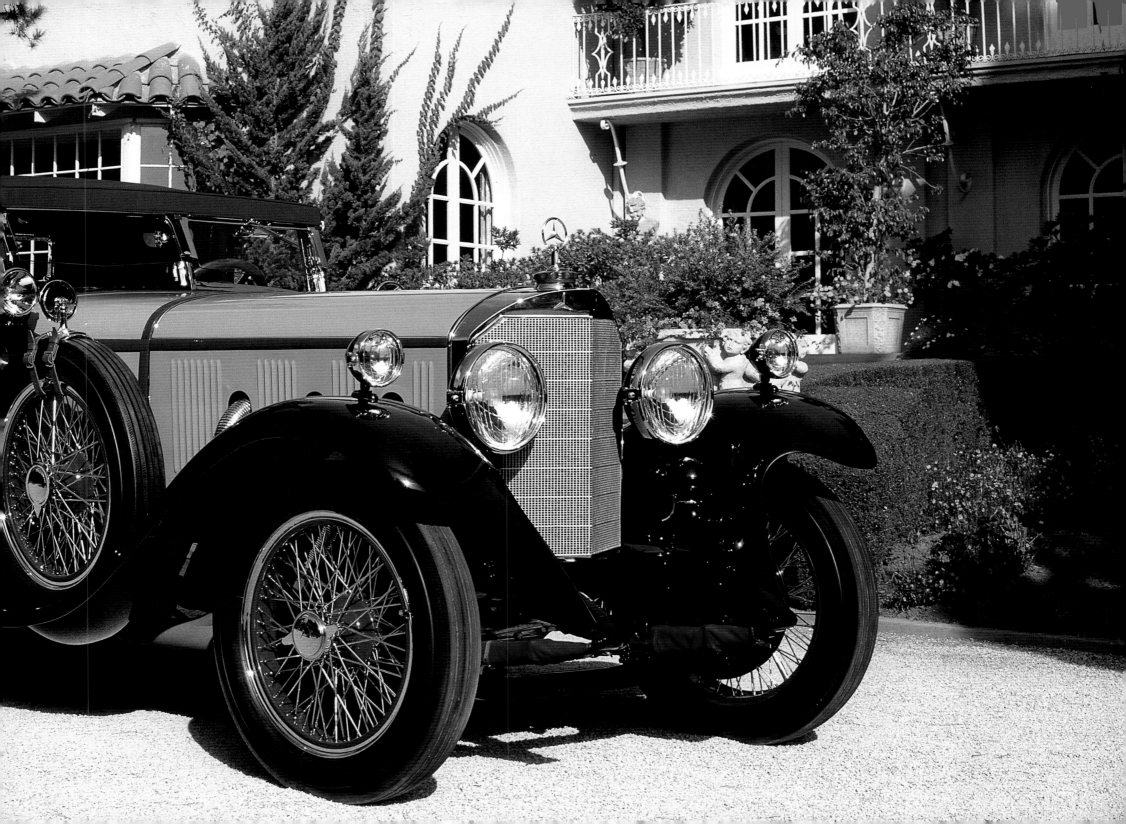

Mercedes-Benz SSK

The boattail design was essentially a French concept pioneered by Paris coachbuilder Henri Labourdette in the early 1910s. Among his earliest achievements was the 1911 Mercedes 37/95 Skiff built for American haberdasher Henry Stetson.

The Labourdette Skiff style launched a thousand imitations in the 1910s, '20s, and '30s. The original design was that of an upright hull with a deck, not the inverted hull (just imagine a canoe turned over) characteristic of American cars such as the Auburn 851 Auburn boattail speedster, Stutz Blackhawk, and Duesenberg French speedster.

One of the earliest examples of an inverted hull design was the 1928 Auburn model 8–115. Designed by Alexis de Sakhnoffsky, one of the leading automotive illustrators and designers of the era, the Auburn established the boattail speedster body style in this country at a time when automobiles sporting such haughty coachwork were rarely found atop an American-made chassis.

The Mercedes-Benz SSK boattail speedster pictured was commissioned in 1928 by Howard Isham of Santa Barbara, California, with the coachwork designed and built by the Walter M. Murphy Company in Pasadena.

As far as can be determined, only one boattail speedster was ever built on an SSK chassis, and of the entire SSK production, roughly 31 cars, only two were bodied outside of Europe and Great Britain; the second, also by Walter M. Murphy, was a Cabriolet built for comedian Zeppo Marx.

A fair number of Model S, SS, and SSK chassis were also done in France by Carrosserie Saoutchik, in England by Freestone and Webb, and in Italy by Carrozzeria Castagna.

For the Isham SSK, Murphy stylists took a similar approach to Labourdette, using an upright hull, but with wider proportions and a flat deck that allowed access to the inside through a locking trunk lid. In many ways this was a more practical design than de Sakhnoffsky's, since the Auburn, with its radically curved boattail, left no appreciable room for either luggage or a spare tire.

Given the dazzling character of the massive Mercedes-Benz grille shell, the enormous trio of exhaust tubes exiting the right side of the hood, and the boldly exposed semi-elliptical frame rails and leaf springs protruding beyond the front apron, there was nothing Murphy could do to change the car's appearance in front of the cowl. Little wonder, then, that so much attention was given to the passenger compartment and rear deck.

Perhaps the raciest-looking SSK ever built, the Murphy boattail was virtually all hood and fenders, with the passenger compartment and boattail deck barely extending beyond the radius of the rear wheels. The only other body style from this era that can even begin to rival the Murphy for the sheer impudence of its design is the famous SSK sport roadster, with an equally exaggerated hood and an impressive stack of spare tires mounted atop the rear deck.

In many ways, Mercedes-Benz, like so many great makes from the classic era, created visual icons that identified its cars, regardless of coachwork. Grilles, of course, were obvious, but Mercedes interiors were also remarkably distinctive. Although instruments could be mounted in any number of configurations by a coachbuilder and in an equally varied selection of dashboard fascias—polished and engine-turned steel, wood veneers, or even leather—the massive, wood-rimmed Mercedes-Benz steering wheel was a true focal point of every SSK interior. It was unmistakable. Murphy worked well around this device, creating a subtle, engine-turned copper fascia to contain the instruments and contrast the interior upholstery

and trim. Polished copper also worked well against the broad, chromed center rim of the steering wheel and the chromed hub, which was emblazoned with the Mercedes star emblem.

The SSK (Super Sport Kurz) was built on a wheelbase measuring just 2,950 mm (approximately 116 inches), some 450 mm (17¾ inches) shorter than the SS chassis. With that as a starting point, Murphy designers concentrated the strength of the bodywork around a small raked windshield and deeply cut down doors, which somehow manage in their abridged dimensions to balance a hood and cowl nearly three-quarters the length of the car! Even more remarkable is that the boattail, which had traditionally been the dominant characteristic in this type of design, took on a role subordinate to the rest of the body unless viewed from the rear, giving the SSK a distinctive appearance either coming or going.

Powered by a 170/225-horsepower (increased to 180/250 horsepower in 1929) Roots supercharged in-line six-cylinder engine displacing 7.65 liters, the SSK was capable of reaching the magic century mark, a speed that, at the time, every builder of luxury cars claimed to achieve; Mercedes actually did.

Mercedes-Benz
540K Special Coupe

With an appearance that one journalist in the 1930s described as showing "aggressive styling and Teutonic arrogance," all Mercedes-Benz
540K models were indeed awe-inspiring. This, however, may well be
the most beautiful 540K ever built. Of the 406 cars produced from
1936 to 1940, only four were bodied as Special Coupes, the most graceful closed car
of the entire classic era. This was the finest design ever to come from the renowned
Daimler-Benz styling studio in Sindelfingen.

The 540K and its predecessors, the 500K and Type 380, all produced in the
1930s, were the first production cars in the world with independent front suspension
by means of parallel wishbones and coil springs. The rear suspension, also independent and also pioneered by Daimler-Benz, utilized a swing-axle design with coil
springs. In the 1930s, this was not a conventional blueprint; most of the automotive
world was still running on solid rear axles and leaf-sprung suspensions.

Powered by a 5.4-liter 180-horsepower supercharged eight-cylinder engine, the
540K was capable of exceeding 100 miles per hour, making it not only one of the
most beautiful but also one of the most powerful automobiles of its time.

Mercedes-Benz

300SL Gullwing

A t the time of its unveiling on February 6, 1954, at New York's International Motor Show, the Mercedes-Benz 300SL took everyone by surprise, particularly the Germans. The car's debut marked the first time in Daimler-Benz history that a new model had been introduced in the United States before it was shown in Germany! This serves to point out just how important the North American market was to Daimler-Benz in the 1950s.

The SL, or *Sehr Leicht,* which translates roughly as "lightweight," was based on the Mercedes-Benz race cars, which had dominated European motorsports in 1952. Having evolved from a competition car, the production version bore many of the same features, including the innovative door design that has become the hallmark of the 300SL. Even though the racing engine and lightweight competition body had to be altered considerably to meet production-car requirements, the fraternal relationship between the cars that had swept the 1952 season and those that would sweep sports-car enthusiasts off their feet throughout the 1950s was unmistakable.

Powered by a six-cylinder engine, the 300SL developed a maximum 215 horsepower (240 horsepower with the sports camshaft), and, at peak performance, could attain 150 miles per hour and go from zero-to-60 in eight seconds, making it the fastest production automobile of its time. Nearly half a century later, it is still the most recognized sports car in the world.

Mercedes-Benz
300SL Roadster

Rarely in automotive history has the introduction of a convertible brought about the demise of the coupé version upon which it was based. However, with the 300SL Roadster, it was a case of succession—the Roadster replaced the Gullwing—and although there will always be great speculation about the reason for the Coupe's termination, it was the opinion of Heinz Hoppe, the Daimler-Benz U.S. representative and later president of Mercedes-Benz of North America, that, in part, it was a result of comments made to Daimler-Benz management by Mercedes importer Max Hoffman.

"A vast majority of the cars went to the States, and Maxie Hoffman told us time and again that his pampered customers wanted a bit more comfort, a larger boot, and a bit more fresh air. In addition, we didn't know how long customers—who can be pretty choosy in this price range—would accept a car so similar to the racing version with all its compromises. That's why we started considering a Roadster offering that extra creature comfort American customers like so much—and the Roadster then went into production in 1957."

Contrary to popular belief, planning for the 300SL Roadster began before the first production Coupes were even delivered. Archive documents indicate that design and construction were to take place beginning in October 1954, with the first Roadster prototype being completed for evaluation by top management in November 1955. The designers of the Gullwing were well aware of its shortcomings from the beginning: no real luggage or trunk area, difficult handling due to the high pivot rear axle, difficult entry and exit due to the high doorsills. The new Roadster would solve these problems. Additionally, they felt an open-model sports car would prove more popular in places like southern California, where 300SL sales were expected to be strong.

In the October 12, 1956, issue of *Collier's*, an article by photojournalist David Douglas Duncan gave readers a sneak peak at the new 300SL.

In the article, Duncan detailed his visit to Germany and Switzerland, where he photographed the new sports car being tested by designer Karl Wilfert. Duncan wrote, "Though much technical data is still cloaked in secrecy, factory officials have released enough details with these exclusive *Collier's* photos to give a clear idea of what that streaking shape really is when standing still. A giant two-seater convertible roadster combining features of Mercedes revolutionary Gullwing-doored 300SL Coupe and the streamlined racer in which Juan Manuel Fangio of Argentina beat the world on the Grand Prix circuit, the World Series of professional racing. The SLS Super Light Special clears the ground by a hand and stands but 33 inches high at the door cowling, lower than the ears of the police dogs assigned to guard it. Designed by racing experts for sportsmen to whom the final product is the only consideration, the 300SLS is unlikely to become the second car in every man's garage. It is meant to be the crown jewel of all sports cars."

When it was introduced at the Geneva Motor Show, Daimler-Benz proudly stated that "the 300 SL Roadster is our response to the demand in many countries for a particularly fast, comfortable, open sports car. This automobile offers a wide range of technical achievements for even greater driving safety and motoring comfort as well as a high standard of practical everyday value for touring in real style."

Though it was not as competitive as the Coupe, the Roadster was the more comfortable and practical of the two 300SL models. The convertible top folded easily and conveniently beneath a hard tonneau that fit flush with the body. A removable hardtop was also available as an option, to give the car a more distinctive look and extra insulation in winter.

The Roadster's improved single-joint swing axle rear suspension, utilizing two

coil springs and a third "compensation" coil spring to reduce swinging movements of the rear suspension, noticeably improved the 300SL's quirky cornering, and, starting with chassis no. 2780 in 1961, Roadsters were fitted with Dunlop disc brakes on all four wheels.

In addition to the changes in the exterior and a new headlight design, the 300SL Roadster came with an entirely new dashboard and instrument panel layout. As to which was better, the Coupe's or the Roadster's, it has become a matter of personal taste among owners: the Coupe's twin round instruments or the Roadster's round dials and new column-style gauges between.

A total of 1,858 Roadsters were delivered between 1957 and 1964. With their conclusion came the end of Mercedes' great postwar era, making the 300SL Coupe and Roadster the most unforgettable German sports cars ever built.

Mercedes-Benz

300Sc Cabriolet

Virtually hand-built to order, the Mercedes-Benz 300S and Sc were far more expensive than any other 300 models, the Sc commanding over $12,500, nearly twice the price of the sporty Gullwing Coupe and more than almost any automobile sold in America. Among the most rare of Stuttgart's early postwar cars, the total in 300S and Sc form came to a mere 760 cars, built between 1952 and 1958. Of the scant 300Sc models produced from September 1955 to April 1958, 98 were Coupes, 53 were Roadsters, and only 49 were Cabriolets, such as this example owned today by Bruce Meyer and originally sold to film star Clark Gable.

The 300Sc, which appeared late in 1955 as a '56 model, introduced sweeping changes to the 300 design, proof that Daimler-Benz was constantly improving its cars, even if it were only going to build 200 of them! The 3.0-liter, six-cylinder overhead-cam engine was now fuel-injected (*Einspritzmotor*) and closely related to the 300SL's, utilizing a Bosch injection pump in place of the S model's three Solex 40 PBIC downdraft carburetors. With a compression ratio increased from 7.8:1 to 8.55:1, the Sc developed 175 horsepower at 5,400 rpm, bettering the S by 25 horses from the same 182.7-cubic-inch displacement. The drive was delivered through a fully synchronized four-speed manual transmission, with either a standard column or sportier floor-mounted shift available. Rear-axle ratios changed with the introduction of the Sc to a lower 4.44:1 from the previous 4.125:1. Fuel injection also increased torque from 170 ft lb to 188 ft lb.

Mercedes-Benz literature of 1956 claimed 200 horsepower from the Sc engine, with a top speed of 112 mph. Despite a curb weight of up to 4,450 pounds, the Sc could deliver its occupants from a stand to 60 mph in a respectable 14 seconds.

Comfort and performance were given greater consideration in the Sc, which introduced a new and more responsive independent rear-suspension design, utilizing a single low-pivot-point rear swing axle with coil springs. As an added convenience on Sc models, a driver-controlled electric motor connected to supplementary torsion bars adjusted the rear suspension's attitude to compensate for the added weight of passengers or luggage.

Aside from the engine changes and the use of larger brake drums to pull the Sc down from speed, the 300S and Sc shared the same specifications of design and were available in similar models: the Cabriolet, Coupe, and Roadster.

Of the two drophead versions, the Cabriolet, with its tall fabric stack and elegantly tailored boot cover, had the more classic lines; the Roadster's top completely disappeared when lowered. All three body styles had a wheelbase of 114.2 inches, an overall length of 185 inches, and a front and rear track measuring 58.2 and 60.0 inches, respectively.

Interior appointments of the 300S and Sc were done in the same fashion as in prewar Mercedes-Benz cars, with plush, roll-and-pleat leather upholstery and fine wood veneers in the buyer's choice of burled or straight-grain walnut lacquered to a glasslike finish.

For the 1950s, the 300Sc, such as this example,

1957 MERCEDES-BENZ 300SC CABRIOLET

offered features precious few automakers even had on their drawing boards: four-wheel fully independent suspension and ventilated bimetal vacuum-assisted brakes, along with a number of safety and convenience features such as backup lights, turn signals, nonglare mirrors, and windshield washers. Inside, there were reclining seats, a signal-seeking radio, and appointments that are still considered luxury options today.

One has only to look at what other automakers had to offer in 1957 to appreciate the 300Sc. In a decade of mass production, when cars were being turned out as quickly as assembly line workers could throw them together, it is almost beyond reason that Mercedes-Benz would build less than 50 examples of a single model. The 300S and Sc marked the passing not only of a style, but of an era. Never again would Mercedes-Benz produce automobiles quite like these.

1957 MERCEDES-BENZ 300SC CABRIOLET

Mercedes-Benz
280SE 3.5 Cabriolet

Daimler-Benz introduced the 280SE 3.5 convertible in the fall of 1969, marking the end of one era in the company's history and the beginning of another with a single car.

The 280SE 3.5 combined the elegant old body styling of the 1960s-era 220SE, hailed as one of the most beautiful automobiles ever built, with an all-new V-8 engine destined to become the standard for the 1970s and beyond. Added to the car's improved performance and inherited luxury was its rarity—only 1,232 were built between 1969 and 1971—making the 280SE 3.5 one of the most sought-after Mercedes-Benz models in recent time—not so rare as to be unobtainable, but few enough in number to be in constant demand.

Although the 3.5 version was to be the last and most luxurious five-passenger convertible to come from Stuttgart (until recent times), its significance in Mercedes-Benz history did not come from styling alone. There was the engine.

Daimler-Benz had placed a remarkably powerful motor behind the 3.5's slightly wider and shorter upright grille shell. Until the 1969 model, the only Mercedes-Benz V-8 available had been the immense 6.3-liter engine used in the refined 600 series pullman limousines and landaulets or to power Mercedes' version of a '60s-era muscle car, the 300 SEL 6.3 sedan. I once saw a 6.3 leave a Pontiac GTO so far behind that the guy thought his engine had stopped running.

With a few exceptions, such as the classic 500K and 540K of the 1930s and the 600 limousines of the 1960s, Daimler-Benz had always managed to fine-tune its four- and

six-cylinder engines to power passenger cars, and though smaller in displacement than the V-8s found in many American automobiles of the period, the Daimler-Benz sixes managed to produce nearly the same power. Thus a new V-8 would have to do something extraordinary.

The 3.5 did.

The new fuel-injected engine compressed the air and gasoline mixture at a ratio of 9.5:1, allowing the compact V-8 to develop a pulse-quickening 230 horsepower, more than one horsepower per cubic inch of displacement. In 1969, those were the kinds of numbers one expected from a Corvette, not a five-passenger touring car! Handily closing the gap between the 3-liter sixes and the 6.3-liter V-8s, the 3.5's

modest dimensions and weight allowed the engine to fit the mature 280SE chassis and provide it with youthful vitality.

Despite a long 110-inch wheelbase, an overall length of 196.2 inches (more than 16 feet), and a weight of 3,640 pounds, the 280SE 3.5 could go from zero-to-60 in just 9.3 seconds and reach an Autobahn-storming speed of 130 mph, performance comparable to that of many European sports cars of the day, and the 3.5 did it with a four-speed automatic transmission.

The 280SE rode atop a fully independent coil-spring suspension with four-wheel disc brakes to reliably scrub off the excess speed that drivers tended to attain with the car.

On the open road and with the top down, the Mercedes avoided the torsional flexing of most open cars by using a strengthened chassis with additional steel cross-braces

below the leading edge of the rear seat, which extended rearward under the trunk. Thus body shudder and cowl shake were virtually nonexistent. And at highway speeds with the top raised, there was nary a flutter in the 1½-inch-thick fabric roof, which took two Daimler-Benz craftsmen 16 hours to build by hand. The 280SE 3.5 Cabriolet rode as quietly as a hardtop coupé.

Taking another page from its classic past, Daimler-Benz stylists endowed the 280SE with an interior one might have expected in a Rolls-Royce. Driver and passengers sat in sumptuous leather-upholstered seats surrounded by polished *wurzelnuss* (walnut root) veneer and every comfort feature available in the 1970s: air-conditioning, reclining front

seatbacks with headrests, a four-speaker Becker Europa AM/FM stereo, and power windows. There was even an optional five-piece set of leather luggage designed to fit snugly into the 3.5's spacious trunk.

Of all the great makes and models to come from Germany in the past 30 years, the 280SE 3.5 Cabriolet was perhaps the most perfect example of a luxury touring car ever built.

This impeccable 1971 model was restored for the Kurt Hillgruber Collection by Mercedes-Benz specialist Jerry Hjeltness.

Mercer Raceabout

Since the turn of the century, and for nearly a decade before, automobilists had been testing the mettle of their motorcars in sporting contests. Most events were intended to establish speed and endurance records not only for the cars but for the drivers, who had little more than a hard seat beneath them and a steel-rimmed steering wheel to grasp hold of. This need to compete, to risk one's life and limb, has been in our blood since the beginning of time, and, in the automotive world of the twentieth century, competition eventually boiled down to one all-encompassing idea—the sports car.

How one defines a sports car depends upon the era in which it was built, and, in the early 1900s, it was built as simply as possible. Early models such as the Mercer Raceabout and Stutz Bearcat were thundering machines comprising little more than two seats attached to a chassis and engine. It was atop cars like these that legendary race drivers Ralph DePalma, Spencer Wishart, and Barney Oldfield built their legendary reputations as daredevil racers.

The Mercer Automobile Company, established in 1910 in Trenton in Mercer County, New Jersey, built what is perhaps the first truly successful American sports car, an automobile that was genuinely ahead of its time in 1911.

The company produced three models: the two-passenger Speedster (later named Raceabout), the five-place Touring (with more substantial coachwork), and the Toy Tonneau four-seater. The Type 35 Raceabout was the New Jersey automaker's most famous car, and, although not endowed with a particularly large engine at just 300 cubic inches, nor exceptional puissance, with the T-head four-cylinder motor managing only 34 horsepower and mounted to a lightweight 116-inch wheelbase chassis with barely any bodywork, it acquitted itself quite nicely on both the open road and the road course.

Mercers were equipped with an unrivaled three-speed selective transmission (later improved to a four-speed in 1913) and an oil-wetted multiple-disc clutch, both of which greatly contributed to the two-seater's brisk acceleration and ability to surpass the benchmark mile-a-minute.

In 1911, Mercer Raceabouts won five out of six major races in which they were entered. The following year, at the Los Angeles Speedway, Ralph DePalma established eight new world records with a Raceabout, and Spencer Wishart took a Model 35 off the showroom floor of an Ohio Mercer dealer and handily won a 200-mile race in Columbus, establishing four new dirt-track records in the process. In 1913, a racing model driven by Wishart finished second in the third running of the Indianapolis 500.

With Mercer, less was more, and the gossamer bodywork of the Raceabout—simply a pair of bucket-type seats, rudimentary fenders, a flimsy hood latched with leather straps and spring clamps, and a stack of spare tires behind the fuel tank—was not an inexpensive purchase. The average price was $2,500, a sobering amount of money in 1911.

The Mercer's sporty, devil-may-care image was not lost on the competition, principally Indianapolis automaker Harry Stutz, whose all-new 1912 Bearcat looked remarkably similar to the 1911 Raceabout and became equally famous in the early 1910s. Independent coachbuilders also began offering Mercer-styled bodies to replace those of the humdrum Model T, and the Raceabout look appeared on early Oakland (later to become Pontiac) models like the 1915 Type 37 Speedster, a more luxurious interpretation of the Mercer and Stutz.

This example of the Mercer Type 35 from the William B. Ruger Sr. collection is one of the earliest cars built of some 150 Raceabouts sold in 1911. Although spartan in design, the car was not lacking in features. The Mercer came with a full complement of brass-framed instruments mounted to the wood firewall, handsome pinstriping on the body—what there was of it—and a tall, polished brass radiator shell.

The Mercer Type 35 has earned its place in the hallowed halls of automotive history, not only as one of the most advanced motor vehicles of the early 1910s, but likely the very first that can honestly be called an American sports car.

Oldsmobile Fiesta

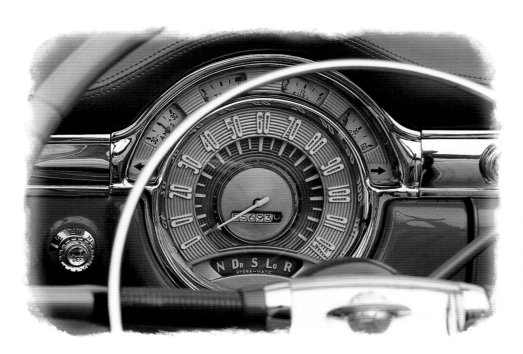

Keeping pace with Cadillac, which offered the exclusive Eldorado as a limited-production model in 1953, Oldsmobile introduced its own special limited-edition luxury convertible—the Fiesta. Originally, it had been a 1952 Auto Show "idea car," showcasing such innovations as the panoramic windshield first used on the Eldorado. But the Fiesta received so much attention that Olds management decided to put it into limited production during the 1953 model year, although it was never pictured in any Oldsmobile sales literature.

Loaded with just about every option in the book, the Fiesta came with a slightly souped-up 170-horsepower version of the Quadri-Jet Rocket V-8, a Hydra-Matic transmission, and a whopping $5,715 price tag, almost twice as much as the base price for an Olds Ninety-Eight convertible. For the money, the Fiesta came with a custom leather-upholstered interior, power steering, power brakes, electric windows, power seats, Autronic-eye automatic headlight dimming, whitewalls, radio, heater, and more. The Fiesta was offered in a choice of four colors. Solids were black and white, with two-tone options in Noel and Nile Green and Surf and Teal Blue. Other combinations were added later in the model year. Only 458 Olds Fiestas were produced, making it one of the rarest postwar American cars.

1953 OLDSMOBILE FIESTA

Packard 5–48

Packard's 1915 Model 5–48 was a fast car. The car wasn't intended to be known for its unsurpassed speed, but it turned out that way just the same. In a 1915 advertisement, Packard's chief engineer, Jesse Vincent, was quoted as saying, "Be careful how you step on this car. It leaps like a projectile."

Introduced in 1912, the Packard Six was offered in a wide variety of body styles. The "48" models were the most expensive yet produced, ranging from $4,850 to $6,550, and the largest motorcars Packard had built since it was founded in 1899.

In 1914 and 1915, the 4–48 and 5–48 series were available on a 12-foot wheelbase (144 inches), with an overall length of 204 inches. Beneath a hood nearly as long as some modern-day cars breathed a massive six-cylinder engine with a swept volume of 525 cubic inches (4½ x 5½–inch bore and stroke) and an output of 80 horsepower, endowing the 5–48 with what Packard called "The Fastest Getaway—60 Miles an Hour in 30 Seconds from a Standing Start." Although that may not sound very impressive today, in 1915 it was a startling speed for anything that wasn't built for racing.

The last of the series, the 5–48, or Fifth 48, set a record at the Indianapolis Motor Speedway, clocking 70 miles in just one hour. The automaker made use of this feat in an advertising campaign that proclaimed the new Packard Dominant Six as the "Boss of the Road," but it was better known in some circles as "Jesse Vincent's Hot Rod."

Being one of the fastest production cars in America, the 5–48 was practically adopted as the official getaway car of the underworld, because it could easily outrun the lower-priced automobiles used by local and state law-enforcement agencies. Noted Packard, "Our friends intimate that the light-

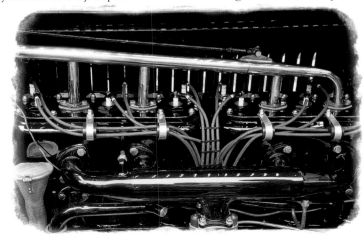

ening like getaway has recommended the Packard to the dark uses of the powers that prey. Jesse James, Dick Turpin and other outlaws of yesterday and the day before used the best horses obtainable. . . . The selection of the Packard by the gun men of New York is, we insist, a matter of evolution and no reflection on the integrity of the car." Still, the notoriety didn't hurt sales.

The 1915 Packard was an impressive-looking automobile, tall in stature, square shouldered, as were most cars of the era, and dignified by a distinctively shaped Packard radiator shell topped by a stylized numeral 6 and a bright-red 48 emblem atop the filler cap. The interesting latch mechanism used on the early Packard radiator caps was the result of lengthy research into a design that would be easy to open and close. As it turned out, the final design was adapted from a Mason jar!

Coachwork for the cars was handcrafted in the Packard body shops, the wood framing and wood trim painstakingly machined and hand-polished in the wood shop. Packards leaving the East Grand Boulevard factory were the epitome of luxury. Regardless of the model, body style, or price, every Packard reflected the same high level of craftsmanship.

This elegant 1915 Model 5–48 seven-passenger Touring from the Nethercutt Collection is painted traditional Packard colors of the era: blue and black, with yellow trim and wheels. The interior is upholstered in top-grain black leather, just as it was in 1915. This stunning open car originally sold for $4,850.

Fast, elegant, well built—85 years later it is still regarded as one of the finest automobiles of its time and worthy of its place among the 100 greatest cars of the twentieth century.

Packard Twin Six

Town Car

If building on the strengths of its prestigious image was the goal, then Packard truly experienced a watershed year in 1915. This was the year the Detroit carmaker stunned the automotive industry with the introduction of the first twelve-cylinder automobile put into series production anywhere in the world, the Twin Six. Designed by Packard's new chief engineer, Jesse Vincent, who joined the firm in 1912, the Twin Six so improved production techniques that the cars sold for less than the previous six-cylinder models! With a base price of only $2,750, Packard had not only built a more refined and more powerful car but had built it for less. At the time of its introduction on May 1, 1915, the Twin Six marked the greatest single advancement in automotive design since the debut of the Mercedes in 1901.

The new V-12 engine actually comprised two banks of L-head cylinders, forming a V at a narrow 60-degree angle. The Twin Six had a swept volume of 424 cubic inches, and a near-silent output of 85 horsepower at 3,000 rpm.

Following Packard's return to commercial automobile production, which had been suspended during World War I to manufacture Liberty aircraft engines, the Twin Six became one of the most prestigious automobiles sold in America. The stately Packards were the car of choice for film stars, industrialists, politicians, and heads of state. In 1921, President-Elect Warren G. Harding rode down Pennsylvania Avenue to the White House in a Twin Six, marking the first time that an automobile was prominently featured in an inaugural parade.

The most successful cars of their time, the big Packards, such as this handsome example from The Nethercutt Collection, were often regarded as "the Rolls-Royces of America." The Twin Six remained in production until 1923, longer than any model up to that time, accounting for a staggering total of 35,000 cars and establishing Packard as one of the world's leading manufacturers of luxury automobiles.

1916 PACKARD TWIN SIX TOWN CAR

Packard Custom
Dietrich V-Windshield Coupe

Among the finest examples of Dietrich styling were the 1933 model 1006 Customs, which, aside from having exquisite exterior styling, featured remarkably advanced interior designs for the period, most notably a sweeping dashboard that wrapped around the driving compartment, seamlessly blending the ends of the instrument panel into the door caps. Then there were Dietrich's rakishly angled V-frame windshields used on models such as this striking 1933 Packard Twelve 1006 Sport Coupe, a design regarded by many as Ray Dietrich's all-time masterpiece.

Despite having designs that stirred car lust in even the most genteel Packard owner, sales in 1933 were not good. The Sport Coupe and companion Sport Phaeton represented a third of the Dietrich designs offered in the Packard custom catalog that year. Dietrich had also penned a stunning Convertible Victoria, Convertible Coupe, Convertible Sedan, and a stately Formal Sedan, which the company drew upon to fill out the year's offerings along with two LeBaron Custom designs on the powerful Packard V-12's 147-inch wheelbase chassis.

The debut of the Tenth Series had been postponed by Packard president Alvan Macauley from August 1932 until January 1933, yet production concluded as usual the following August, making 1933 one of the shortest model years in Packard history. And it was just as well; sales were off the pace as the Depression deepened and even those with the money to purchase a new Packard Custom did not—some just being conservative, others waiting to see if the administration of newly elected President Franklin Delano Roosevelt could change the economic tide that had swept wealth and prosperity from every corner of the nation.

In spite of the Depression, Packard still did well in 1933, delivering a total of 4,800 cars, earning a very modest profit of $506,433 on $19,230,000 in sales, $6,000 of which came from this lone Series 1006 Dietrich Sport Coupe, the only example built in 1933.

Owner Ronald Benach has traced the history of this one-off Dietrich coupe back to millionaire John Mecom. The car was purchased new by Mecom and remained in his family for some 25 years until Houston, Texas, collector Charles Worthen purchased the car in the late 1950s. Worthen kept the rare Dietrich Packard for almost 40 years, making Benach only its third owner.

A rare combination of elegance and dazzling style—subtle, yet impossible to overlook—the Dietrich Sport Coupe, with its long hood, V-windshield frame, and beautifully sculptured roofline, remains one of the most dazzling closed cars ever built, a hallmark of Ray Dietrich's 1930s styling, and truly one of the 100 greatest automobiles of all time.

Packard Twelve
1107 Coupe Roadster Convertible Sedan

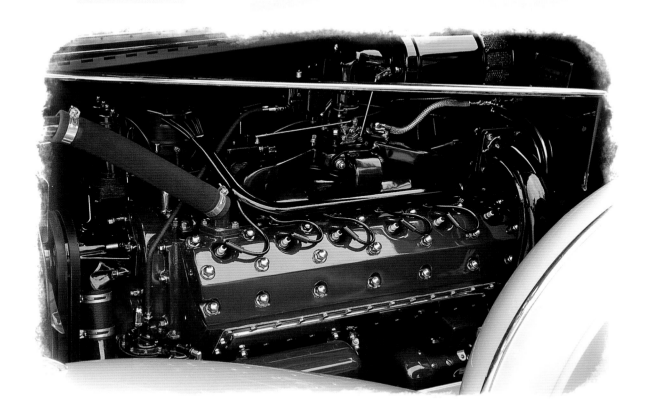

One of the eleven Dietrich body designs for Packard's 1934 semicustom line, this 1107 Packard Twelve Coupe Roadster from the collection of Dr. Joseph A. Murphy was one of the most attractive and sportiest American cars of the 1930s. It was Raymond Dietrich's desire to design convertibles that looked as good with the tops up as down and, in many instances, better with the top up, because that is how most were ultimately driven. Packard offered 10 paint colors in 1934, including this striking shade of silver. The Packard Twelve was one of the most powerful engines offered in the 1930s and second only to Marmon's V-16 for cubic-inch displacement. In 1934, the 455.5 cubic-inch Packard delivered 160 horsepower.

1934 PACKARD TWELVE 1107 COUPE ROADSTER CONVERTIBLE SEDAN

Packard Dietrich
Special Sport Sedan "Car of the Dome"

For Packard, the Dietrich signature on a coachbuilt body had become a symbol of exceptional quality. This was ironic in a sense, because the man whose name meant so much to Packard's wealthiest clientele had been working for Chrysler Corporation as head of exterior design since 1931. The body designs used throughout the early 1930s were all penned by Dietrich prior to his departure to Walter P. Chrysler's side of town and formed the basis of the most dramatically styled Packards in years. The most important of these became the centerpiece of the 1933 Chicago World's Fair Century of Progress Exposition—the Dietrich Style 3182 Special Sport Sedan. The car was chosen by Packard to demonstrate how important sedans were to the company's luxury image. As it would turn out, this was one of the most important decisions Packard management would make in 1933.

Built along the waterfront of Lake Michigan, the Chicago Exposition's architecture was a brilliant montage of color and form, the latest in art deco, modern, and contemporary designs. It was there, under the giant dome of the Travel and Transportation Building, which rose a majestic 12 stories above the fairgrounds, that an art jury was asked to designate one automobile to represent the epitome of motorcar transportation. They did not choose a sporty phaeton or speedster but the elegant Dietrich sedan.

Later known as the "Car of the Dome," the bronze 1933 Packard featured a low roofline, V'd windshield, and sweeping fenders, accentuated by stylist Alexis de Sakhnoffsky's famed false hood, which gave the car the appearance of added length by eliminating the cowl and taking the hoodline all the way back to the windshield.

The Dietrich Packard was selected not only for its exterior styling but for its interior design and appointments as well.

"Aside from its unique lines, this Packard is of special interest because of the costliness of its interior furnishings," noted factory literature accompanying the display. "All

body hardware is heavily gold plated and so are the steering column and instruments. Wood paneling and trim are highly polished burled Carpathian elm. Built into the back of the front seat is a cabinet extending the full width of the car. The right side is occupied by a full length dressing case with gold plated fittings. At the left is a cellaret with a drop door which becomes a glass covered table when lowered. Upholstery is especially selected beige broadcloth. The exterior finish is called Sun Glow Pearl, a new finish which is gold, brown, or pearl, depending upon how the light strikes it."

Although its design was completely new for 1933, the car was updated in August to reflect new fender, bumper, and cowl vent styling for the coming model year. A Packard crew came in and made the changes overnight, so that, when the World's Fair opened the next day, the car had all of the new styling cues for 1934.

In an academic sense, this was perhaps the most important car in Packard's history. At the time of the Chicago World's Fair, the automobile as a concept and recognized mode of personal transportation in this country was barely 40 years old, yet, among all of the cars available in 1933—Duesenbergs, Cadillacs, Lincolns, Marmons, and Pierce-Arrows, to name just a few—this stunning 12-cylinder Packard sedan was the one chosen to represent the automobile in its grandest form.

Packard Darrin

American Howard "Dutch" Darrin had been designing custom coachwork in Paris, France, since 1922, where he had established Hibbard & Darrin Carrossier with friend and fellow designer Thomas Hibbard.

Darrin's first independent designs had been completed a year earlier, on a pair of Delage chassis Dutch purchased from Walter P. Chrysler. He designed his own custom bodies for the cars and sold one of them to screen star Al Jolson, thus beginning a lifelong career as the coachbuilder to the stars.

After Hibbard returned to the United States in 1932, Darrin formed a new partnership with a wealthy Paris banker named Fernandez. Through 1937, Fernandez & Darrin produced some of the most acclaimed custom coachwork of the era for film stars, monarchs, and industrialists.

Darrin finally returned to the United States at the beckoning of film producer Darryl Zanuck. Darrin was also friends with actors Errol Flynn, Chester Morris, and Clark Gable, and they helped convince him that he could do better building custom-bodied cars in the United States. In 1937 he returned to Southern California, where he set up a coachbuilding facility in an old bottle factory located at 8860 Sunset Boulevard. It was known as Darrin of Paris, and the Hollywood film colony flocked to his door.

He sold the first example of what would come to be known as a "Hollywood Darrin" to film star Dick Powell in 1938. Within a year, Dutch had built cars for Clark Gable, Tyrone Power, Errol Flynn, Chester Morris, Ruby Keeler, Ann Sheridan, Preston Foster, and Gene Krupa, among others.

Darrins were considerably different from the more refined and contemporary coachwork offered by the Packard factory. Some of the styling changes made by Darrin were simple yet quite effective. For example, the rear fenders were removed, slightly stretched, and then rehung with a forward slant, while the front fenders were restyled and skirted to fit a body absent of running boards. The radiator shell was cut down by three inches, and the hood was sectioned. The Hollywoods were also fitted with custom-built windshield frames, and Dutch's favorite modification, cut-down, suicide-style doors.

"The very early cars," said Darrin shop foreman Rudy Stoessel, "were not like the later ones. The first two still had running boards. We built one for Clark Gable and another for Chester Morris," better known as fictional film detective Boston Blackie. The construction of the first Darrins was pretty makeshift. Clark Gable once said of Dick Powell's car that it "looks better the farther you get away from it."

Darrin interiors featured a new idea, a padded dashboard, which was favored by Dutch not only for its handsome appearance but inherent safety. Well ahead of its time, the Darrin padded dash extended across the entire width of the driver's compartment and continued around into the tops of the doors, giving driver and passenger a soft armrest when the windows were lowered.

Although, between 1937 and 1939, only 16 custom-bodied Packards were produced at the Sunset Strip shop, it seemed as though every film star in Hollywood was driving one, which led Packard to take up production of the cars in 1940. The Packard Darrins were built at the old Auburn automobile assembly plant in Connersville, Indiana. Around 50 victorias, a dozen convertible sedans, and three sport sedans were produced between 1940 and 1942, earning the Darrin-designed cars the distinction of being among the rarest of all Packard models.

Packard
One-Eighty Clipper

As Packard's director of design, Ed Macauley needed someone to come up with an all-new model for 1941. Macauley, who was the son of Packard chairman Alvan Macauley, had surrounded himself with the best talent available outside of Harley Earl's Art and Color Section at General Motors. In addition to Packard chief stylist Werner Gubitz (who apprenticed under Ray Dietrich in the 1920s and joined Packard in 1930), he had John Reinhart (later to design the Continental Mk II for Ford), Phil Wright (designer of the 1933 Pierce-Arrow Silver Arrow), Howard Yeager, and Ed Nowacky.

Macauley's father and Packard's legendary chief engineer, Jesse Vincent, both suggested that he hedge his bets by going outside the styling studio to commission proposals from independent designers. Macauley engaged John Tjaarda and Alex Tremulis of the Briggs Body Company to work up a proposal of their own for a new model, along with independent designers George Walker (later of Ford Thunderbird fame) and Bill Flajole. This was a brain trust that would have made any automaker beam with pride, but Ed Macauley had one more name to draw out of his hat: Howard Dutch Darrin.

Macauley contacted Darrin and offered him $1,000 a day if he could come up with a new design in 10 days. The reason for the sudden urgency, and the incredible amount of money offered, is not known. The irony of the thing, as Dutch lamented many years later, was that he never got paid for the design, which he did, in fact, complete in 10 days. Because Packard was Darrin's largest client, there was

very little he could do about it. Orders for the custom-built Darrin Packards were increased as a kind of backhanded remuneration, and that would have been fine, but, before they were put into production, Packard canceled the order!

Darrin had a long-standing reputation for designing custom bodies that attracted attention, and what Macauley needed now was a production car that would do the same thing. Dutch gave it to him—literally. Macauley came out to California, picked up Darrin's proposal in the form of a quarter-scale clay model, and took it back to Detroit. That was the last Dutch ever saw of it until the 1941 Clipper was introduced.

In little more than a week's time, Dutch Darrin accomplished what no one had been able to do for Packard in more than a decade: create a car that was completely

new yet unmistakably a Packard. A bold departure from traditional styling, the Clipper was 12 inches greater in width than in height, making it the widest and lowest passenger car then in production, and the Clipper's lower roofline was not at the expense of interior headroom. Just as GM designer Bill Mitchell had done to achieve a lower roofline with the 1938 Cadillac Sixty Special, the Clipper was built on a double drop frame, which brought the floorpan closer to the ground, allowing interior dimensions to remain unchanged while rendering a noticeably lower and sleeker exterior line.

The Clipper's body construction also broke new ground in 1941. Unlike previous designs, which had utilized separate pieces for much of the body, the Clipper's exterior panels were largely made up of individual stampings. The hood, grille, and

1942 PACKARD ONE-EIGHTY CLIPPER

each quarter panel were formed from single sheets of steel, and the entire roof was a single stamping from the windshield back to the decklid.

A midyear entry, Clippers did not start arriving in dealer showrooms until April 1941. Only available as a four-door sedan, it was an immediate success. In the first year, which for the Clipper was only seven months, 16,600 cars were sold, with a base price of $1,375. This represented a sizable percentage of 1941 model year sales for Packard, which sold a total of 72,855 cars.

The 1942 model year began in August of '41, and with it Packard expanded the Clipper line to include One-Sixty and One-Eighty series sedans, a new One-Eighty Fastback (designed in-house by Packard), and lower-priced Clipper Six and Clipper Eight models.

The new One-Eighty Clipper, such as the model pictured from the collection of Neil Torrence, offered one of the most powerful production engines available in America in 1942, Packard's 356-cubic-inch, 165-horsepower straight eight. Overall, the Clipper was the most stunning new car Americans had seen in years, but its future was doomed. The new Packards had barely arrived in dealer showrooms when Japan attacked Pearl Harbor and America was plunged into World War II. On February 9, 1942, after selling more than 46,000 Clippers in less than two years, Packard joined the rest of the American automotive industry in the war effort by suspending civilian automobile production.

It took more than 12 months for Packard to get back into production after the war, and, by then, the magnificent 1941–42 Clipper was an old design. It was replaced in the fall of 1947 by one of worst-looking cars Packard ever built. In all fairness, the One-Eighty Clippers were the finest prewar American cars of the 1940s, and that's a tough act to follow.

Packard Caribbean

Packard was a troubled company in the 1950s, a company that had lost not only its direction but the patronage of its once loyal customers. Under the guidance of newly appointed president James J. Nance, the former head of Hotpoint and one of the highest-profile corporate executives in America, the Detroit automaker began an arduous restructuring, which would ultimately prove to be too little, too late. In the interim, though, one new model did briefly reclaim the magic of Packard's prewar luxury car image, the 1953–54 Caribbean.

The all-new 1953 model line was the first publicly recognized achievement under Nance, spearheaded by the stylish, limited-production Caribbean. Powered by Packard's tried-and-true straight-eight engine, the cars were practically hand-built, and, in 1953 and '54, they re-ignited the flame at East Grand Boulevard that had once burned so brightly.

The Caribbean's styling was rooted in the 1952 Packard Pan American show car. Designed by a former General Motors stylist, Richard Arbib of the Henney Motor Company in Freeport, Illinois, the Pan American was adapted from a leftover 1951 production Packard convertible. Arbib had the body sectioned four inches to provide a lower silhouette; the windshield, radiator, steering column, and suspension were also lowered to contribute to the ground-hugging effect. To give it the look of a sports car, although on a somewhat larger scale, the rear seat was removed and the area enclosed with a metal tonneau cover. A functional air scoop was added to the hood and a trendy continental kit mounted for the spare tire.

To everyone's surprise, the Pan American was the hit of the 1952 New York Auto Show. Dealers and customers flooded East Grand with requests for a production version, and Packard found itself with an unexpected winner. The car had stirred public interest and sales momentum that Packard could ill afford to lose in the toughly competitive postwar Fifties. To test the waters further, management approved the construction of five more Pan Americans for the show-car circuit

before considering actual production. The result was the same wherever the cars appeared, and, by spring of 1952, Nance had authorized a production version, to be based on the upcoming 1953 convertible designed by Packard's new chief stylist, Richard Teague. Like the show cars, this too would have to be a rush job, ready for debut in less than a year.

Mired in its own production problems, Packard contracted with the Mitchell-Bentley Company of Ionia, Michigan, to convert 750 standard '53 Packard convertibles into a limited run of "personal sports cars," which were introduced as the Packard Caribbean and followed in 1954 by another 400 cars of similar, though more luxurious, design. The Caribbeans were a success, but a single model could not save the foundering Packard Motor Car Company.

The Caribbean name was continued in 1955 and 1956, the last two years of true Packard production, but the cars were standard-body convertibles, with no resemblance to either the Pan American or earlier Caribbeans.

By 1957, Packard had been taken over by Studebaker, and the cars from East Grand Boulevard were no more. The '53 Caribbean had been the company's last, best hope. Almost half a century later, it is the model around which Packard enthusiasts gather to remember the final days of America's greatest independent automaker.

Pierce-Arrow

Silver Arrow

Odd as it may sound, the futuristic 1933 Pierce-Arrow Silver Arrow show car originated in the Art and Color Section of General Motors! It was there that a talented young designer named Phil Wright began work on what he called an aerodynamic coupe, and, had it not been for the Depression, the stylish Silver Arrow might have been seen for the first time on the Cadillac display stand at the 1933 New York Auto Show instead of Pierce-Arrow's. Wright, however, fell victim to a belt-tightening at GM in 1932 and, before completing the design, found himself an unemployed stylist with a great idea.

His sudden dismissal turned out to be a blessing for Wright. Holding the drawings he had worked on at General Motors, he paid a visit to his friend Roy Faulkner. Back in 1929, when Faulkner was one of E. L. Cord's top executives, he had hired Wright to design a show car on the L–29 Cord chassis. Now Faulkner was vice president of sales for Pierce-Arrow, and Wright thought he might be able to sell his design to the prestigious New York automaker.

When Wright unrolled the renderings across Faulkner's desk, the Pierce-Arrow execu-tive saw what he considered to be the future of the automobile—a sleek, aerodynamic shape unlike any car's then in production. He hired Wright on the spot and immediately sent him to Pierce's parent company, Studebaker, in South Bend, Indiana, to begin work on a prototype. Working with Studebaker's chief body designer, Jimmy Hughes, Wright penned the final details of what was to become the 1933 Silver Arrow.

The South Bend styling department produced the first car from drawings in a total of only eight weeks! Of course, to accomplish this, a crew of 30 craftsmen worked day and night on the second floor of Studebaker's engineering building. The Silver Arrows were assembled by hand, with the body panels pounded into shape over hardwood hammer forms and then welded to the body framework. On New Year's Day 1933, the first 12-cylinder Pierce-Arrow Silver Arrow was ready for delivery to the New York Auto Show. Thereafter, Silver Arrows were finished every 12 days until a total of five had been built. The second, fourth, and fifth cars were dispatched to Pierce-Arrow headquarters in Buffalo, New York. The third was sent to the Century of Progress exhibition in Chicago, where it vied for attention with Ray Dietrich's stunning Packard Twelve "Car of the Dome," Harley Earl's V-16 Cadillac Aero-Dynamic Coupé, and Gordon Buehrig's stunning Duesenberg Twenty Grand sedan, which also happen to be three of the 100 greatest cars of this century.

Of the five Silver Arrow show cars, only three exist today. The Silver Arrows brought about a styling renaissance at Pierce-Arrow, pioneering designs that would later became industry standards. First to catch the eye were the flush fenders, with a hinged portion to conceal the spare tire. In true Pierce-Arrow fashion, the headlights were faired into the fenders, and the streamlined body had recessed door handles, concealed running boards, rear fender skirts, and a tapered, fastback roofline. Not sur-prisingly, the Pierce-Arrow exhibit was continually crowded with spectators, drawn by

the automaker's claim of giving "the American public a concrete vision of the automobile of the future."

In 1934, Pierce-Arrow introduced a production version of the Silver Arrow, and, although the New York automaker didn't adopt all of the innovative designs, its similarity to the show cars was unmistakable. The Silver Arrow was superior in many ways, making the 1934 model one of the few instances in automotive history when the sequel was even better than the original.

Although the production model wasn't quite the thing of beauty the show car had been, it came very close, with a sloping fastback roof design, V-shaped rear window,

and the general streamlining of the 1933 prototypes. The production Silver Arrows were offered with either the big Pierce V-12 engine or a smaller, more affordable straight eight. The V-12 sold for $3,895, the eight for $3,495.

Although highly praised for its innovative design, the Silver Arrow's influence on automotive styling was not immediate. In the midst of the Great Depression, the majority of American automakers were too busy just trying to keep their heads above water to embrace any of the car's radical new design theories. Eventually, most of the styling tenets proposed by Pierce-Arrow's four-wheeled crystal ball came to pass. Unfortunately, by then Pierce-Arrow was long gone.

1933 PIERCE-ARROW SILVER ARROW

Porsche

Gmünd Limousine

Just prior to Germany's invasion of Poland, Professor Ferdinand Porsche, his son Ferdinand "Ferry" Porsche Jr., and chief stylist Erwin Franz Komenda created a sleek aerodynamic coupé body to fit the Volkswagen platform designed by Professor Porsche. Known as the Type 64 (K6010), three prototypes were built with the intention of campaigning them in the 1939 Berlin-to-Rome event. With the onset of war, the race was canceled. Two of the cars remained with Porsche KG; the third was badly damaged in a crash and left behind when the factory moved from Zuffenhausen to the small Austrian village of Gmünd. It was here, in 1947, inside a converted sawmill, that Ferry Porsche, engineer Karl Rabe, and designer Erwin Komenda laid the groundwork for the first car to bear the Porsche name.

The project was officially named the Type 356. In his design, Ferry Porsche used Volkswagen steering and braking systems, suspensions, transmissions, and engines with slight modifications. Developed in parallel with a roadster, the 356/2 limousine utilized a newly designed frame, and, following the design his father had created for the Volkswagen in 1938, Ferry placed the engine behind the rear axle. This was to become the basic Porsche configuration. Completed in July 1948, the car was dubbed the Gmünd Limousine (Coupé). It was a simple two-place sports car powered by a modified VW flat-four engine. The coupé featured a classic fastback roof design similar to the experimental Type 64 race cars. Example pictured, owned by former Porsche dealer Chuck Stoddard, was the sixth car completed in Austria. Stoddard's car is an actual Gmünd body, and aside from the Gmünd roadster in the Porsche museum, it is the lowest serial number car still known to exist of approximately 46 cars built between 1948 and 1950.

Porsche Speedster

The original 356 Speedster, added to the Porsche line in September 1954 as a 1955 model, was built for a purpose few Americans in the early 1950s truly understood. Those who did flocked to Max Hoffman's Park Avenue dealership in New York City and signed up for the handful of cars being imported into this country.

Everyone who has ever owned a Speedster or dreamed of owning one remembers the car fondly, despite the fact that these early Porsches were very noisy, their VW-derived suspensions rudimentary at best and, unless one had some modicum of driving skill and knew how to *throw* them around corners, treacherous to drive at the limit. The Speedster was the closest thing to a race car you could put on the street in 1955. Not terribly fast but with almost no insulation and riding just inches above the pavement, in the Speedster even 60 mph felt like you were racing down the wind.

The Speedster bore Porsche's traditional "bathtub" styling, a slightly hump-backed appearance with sweeping fenderlines and downward-sloping doors. Inside, however, Speedsters were distinguished from other 356 models by a low, curved windshield, a unique instrument panel with three gauges shrouded by a rounded binnacle, and a wide stretch of dashboard painted body color. There was no glovebox, only the lone Porsche script and an angled grab handle on the passenger's side. The most lavish feature was the dash top, neatly upholstered to match the seats and door panels. Purchasers had the choice of vinyl or leather upholstery for the stylish lightweight bucket seats but few other options. The Speedster was a no-frills car. There was no provision for a radio, no ashtray or cigarette lighter, and the flat door panels were without storage pockets.

The Speedster was a stripped car, commensurately priced at only at $2,985. It was an unpretentious sports car for the few and, as it turned out, perhaps too few. Hoffman's pipeline filled quickly. From the start, Ferry Porsche had been skeptical of the Speedster's appeal, saying, "stripping a car only degrades it, without achieving the intended result." Although early Speedster aficionados may beg to differ, the fact remains that sales proved Dr. Porsche correct. Hoffman, however, was also right, because the Speedster attracted attention, and, when a customer complained of the spartan interior, it was only a short step up to the more refined and luxuriant 356 Cabriolet. Still, there were those who found the little 356 ideal, and, by 1958, Speedsters, such as this example originally owned and raced by actor Steve McQueen, were being campaigned from coast to coast in sports car club competition.

Originally fitted with the plain-bearing 1,500, 1,500S (a $500 option), 1,300 Normal, or 1,300 Super engines, the Speedster later became available with two versions of the pushrod 1,600 engine and four-cam Carrera engine, in 1955. The ultimate Speedster was the four-cam Carrera GS GT, introduced in November 1955.

Sadly, the era of the true Speedster was short-lived. By 1958 Porsche had completed the design for a more civilized Speedster that would go into production in August of that year; thus 1958 marked the end of a brief but wonderful era at Porsche. Along with such legendary cars as the Mercedes-Benz 300SL and Jaguar XKE, the Speedster has become timeless, a car whose luster has not dulled in over four decades.

Porsche 901/911

It has been more than 35 years since the Porsche 911 was introduced, yet the original profile and design of the car has endured, confirming a very simple, though difficult-to-achieve tenet of design; in simplicity there is beauty. The 911 was designed by Ferdinand Alexander "Butzi" Porsche, grandson of the company's founder. Showing a remarkable talent for styling, Butzi, who joined the family business in 1957, apprenticed under his grandfather's chief stylist, Erwin Franz Komenda, the former deputy director of passenger car design at Daimler-Benz.

After the success of the 356, which had been in production since 1948, Butzi approached the redesign of the only model the company had ever built with some reluctance. Unlike Ford or General Motors, where an unsuccessful model could be swept under the carpet, a miscalculation on the 356's successor could have spelled disaster for the small, family-owned company.

Already an accomplished designer by the age of 28, when he became head of the styling department at Porsche, Butzi was willing to bend, if not rewrite, the rules of established Porsche design, and, by 1961, he had finalized the bodylines and engineering for the aging 356's successor.

The problem Butzi had to address from the very beginning of the project was one of propriety. "Must you build a new Porsche just like the old one," as his mentor Komenda had suggested, or was there another approach? In many respects, the answer was yes to both questions. In his final analysis of the 911 project Butzi wrote, "It should be a new Porsche . . . as good or better than the old, and in the same

pattern, but not necessarily the same form." A somewhat enigmatic statement, but easily understood when looking at the 911, a virtual extension of the 356 design—longer, sleeker, more powerful, but quintessentially Porsche. Butzi had accomplished what no one, even the legendary Komenda, had been able to do—recreate the Porsche in its own image.

The 911 embodied more changes than the company had ever made, from the body and interior right down to the final suspension layout and new overhead cam, six-cylinder boxer engine—the foundation of every 911 motor to the present day, even the all-new water-cooled 911 engine.

The Porsche 911 measured up as both a larger and a smaller car compared to its predecessor. The wheelbase was longer to provide additional footroom, larger rear seats, and longer doors to allow easier entry and exit. The upper body was wider to increase hip and shoulder room, while the passing of the 356's "bathtub" physique allowed the sleek 901's exterior to *decrease* in width by almost three inches. From end to end, the 901 was some five inches greater in length than the 356.

By any account, the 911 was a stunning success, continuing the Porsche tradition while at the same time creating a new following—a cadre of owner/enthusiasts who have made the 911 the most successful production sports car in automotive history.

The source Porsche, the car featured, is one of the original 901/911 prototypes built in 1963, and is recognized today as the oldest surviving 911 in the world. Completely restored, it is owned by Porsche collector Don Meluzio.

1963 PORSCHE 901/911

Rolls-Royce
Silver Ghost

S ome roads in Scotland haven't been improved since the days of William Wallace. One in particular is called Rest and Be Thankful; after ascending this roughhewn two-mile trail, cut through a strikingly green valley that hasn't changed in more than a century, one can indeed appreciate the brevity of the name. You need to rest at the top, and you're surely thankful that your car didn't blow a tire off the rim, overheat, or simply run afoul on the tortuous incline. Back in June 1907, Claude Johnson, the commercial managing director of Rolls-Royce, Ltd., drove the very first Silver Ghost up Rest and Be Thankful in the Scottish Reliability Trial.

Known to have a penchant for showmanship, especially when the press was in attendance, Johnson had taken the Silver Ghost up the grueling slope a month earlier for a comparison test against a White steam car and had negotiated the final hairpin turn at the hilltop four additional times, twice in reverse, for the benefit of a London *Times* photographer! In June, Johnson and the Silver Ghost completed the 774-mile Scottish Reliability Trial again without incident, winning the Gold Medal for excellence in hill climbing, reliability, and fuel consumption. It was a monumental accomplishment at a time when the motorcar was considered to be a plaything for the upper class.

Ninety years later, Rolls-Royce took the very same car back to Scotland and traversed Rest and Be Thankful once again, and again without incident! For the superbly maintained 90-year-old car, built when Teddy Roosevelt was president of the United States, this was a historic moment. The Silver Ghost and the Scottish countryside were the same as they had been in 1907; only the people had changed.

This particular car was actually the thirteenth 40–50 horsepower chassis built by Rolls-Royce, serial number 60551, and, up until that time, the model was simply

216

1907 ROLLS-ROYCE SILVER GHOST

cataloged by the horsepower rating. It had no name nor had the famous Spirit of Ecstasy hood ornament been created for Rolls-Royce by sculptor Charles Sykes. That wouldn't come until 1910.

When Claude Johnson saw the beautiful *Roi-de-Belges* Open Touring body that had been built for 60551 in London by Barker, coachmakers to the royal family, he decided it should have a proper name and, after some deliberation, christened it the Silver Ghost, which became the popularly accepted designation for all subsequent 40–50 horsepower models. "Silver, as being pure and hallmarked, and Ghost, as being symbolic of its smooth, silent, effortless movement," wrote Johnson, who commissioned a repoussé nameplate for 60551 that still adorns the car's scuttle.

His definitions of the Silver Ghost's performance in 1907 are still appropriate nine decades later. After starting the engine with one or two turns of the hand crank, the 7-liter in-line six still comes to life with a near-silent chuff, running so smoothly that there is barely a trace of movement in the body at idle. Even under full throttle, the engine scarcely makes a sound; there is just the rush of wind blowing past as the Silver Ghost gathers speed.

The sheer elegance of this car has made it as timeless as its achievements. Back in July and August 1907, the Silver Ghost established a new record for reliability, covering 15,000 miles, driven day and night (except on Sundays) without a breakdown or unscheduled stop. Beginning July 1, Johnson had covered nearly a third of the distance before handing off the car to the Honorable C. S. Rolls, Eric Platford (one of Royce's original apprentices), and Reginald Macready. Johnson took the wheel again to finish the run on Thursday, August 8, 1907, and there, amongst much fanfare and cheers, made a theatrical gesture of turning off the engine for the press. It was

done. The world record of 7,089 miles had been broken, better than doubled.

Although this achievement would have thrilled any automaker, at the end of the trial, Johnson turned over the keys to the Royal Auto Club (RAC), which was charged with the task of completely dismantling and inspecting the car for engine, transmission, brake, or steering wear. Their report showed that, except for routine maintenance performed during the five-week-long endurance run and the replacement of tires, the Silver Ghost showed no measurable wear. The RAC concluded, "Had the car been in the hands of a private owner no replacements would have been considered necessary." The summer of 1907 had made Rolls-Royce the most talked-about automaker in the world and the Silver Ghost the most famous automobile of its time.

In 1908, Johnson authorized the sale of the Silver Ghost to A. M. (Dan) Hanbury, one of Rolls-Royce's traveling inspectors. During his ownership, it accumulated more than half a million miles!

Following Hanbury's death in 1947, the car was repurchased from his estate by Rolls-Royce, Ltd., and restored for the first time in its history. The refitting was done in stages over several years and the car assigned to the Public Affairs Department for use at auto shows, in public displays, and commemorative events. Over the last 50 years, it has been kept in pristine condition, given a second restoration in 1988 by the renowned British firm of P. & A. Wood, and, along the way, accumulated another 200,000 miles.

Though more than 90 years and more than 700,000 miles have passed beneath its wheels, the Silver Ghost remains the essence of Sir Henry Royce's heroic creed: *Quidus recte factum quamuis humile praeclarum*. "Whatsoever is rightly done, however humble, is noble."

Rolls-Royce
Springfield Silver Ghost

The year was 1920, at the dawn of an era that would come to be known as "the Roaring Twenties," a decade that would lead America out of the post–World War I recession and into a period of economic and social prosperity that would seem to never end.

It did.

On October 28, 1929, the value of U.S. securities lost $26 billion, a figure that even today would have shocking repercussions. In 1929, it was devastating. In one day, all that seemed bright dimmed, and everyone wondered what would happen next, from the executives in their skyscraper offices to the working-class people on the streets below. Aside from those who lost their fortunes in a single day, the aftermath of Black Friday wasn't truly felt for several years. By then, this stunning 1921 Rolls-Royce Silver Ghost was a decade old, almost a relic compared to the stunning designs being offered to those who could still afford the price of a bespoke suit, an apartment in Manhattan, and a luxurious car. Still, even in the shadows of Phantoms, this was a Ghost of uncommon character, one unlike any that had preceded it.

From around 1915 on, the sporty coachwork that had been appearing on models like Mercer and Stutz, Mercedes, Benz, Alfa Romeo, and Hispano-Suiza was encouraging designers the world over to take bold new steps in the styling of custom coachwork. For the traditionalists at Rolls-Royce in Derby, however, these changes were almost unthinkable, improper, in fact, for the stateliest of motorcars. In 1920, that wasn't what American designers were thinking when R. W. Schuette, Esquire, the Rolls-Royce representative in New York City, called on Rolls-Royce of America, Inc., in Springfield, Massachusetts, with a customer order in hand for a Silver Ghost runabout. A Rolls-Royce roadster? The very idea intrigued the Springfield staff because this body design had never been attempted on a chassis as large as the Silver Ghost's

144-inch wheelbase. It would either be a benchmark design for the American branch or a colossal gaff that would give the gentlemen at the club in England something to talk about.

Of course, there had been sporting coachwork produced for Rolls-Royce chassis since the prestigious British automaker first introduced the Silver Ghost in 1907, but nothing had been as rakish in appearance or as bold a departure from traditional styling as this. The result was surprisingly handsome, allowing a customary-length Rolls-Royce hood; spacious and luxuriously appointed passenger compartment, albeit just for two; and a folding companion, or "trap," seat in the well-proportioned rear deck. Not only was it attractive, the design was so well received that it ostensibly became the prototype for the famed Rolls-Royce Piccadilly Roadsters.

When the chassis for this car arrived from England aboard the S.S. *Vennonia* on March 30, 1921, the Springfield works had less than three months to build the body, which had to be ready for the customer no later than the third week of July. Arriving in the white, the chassis was first painted the same shade of green that was proposed for the body, and American instruments with the Rolls-Royce name on them were fitted to the dash.

Because a runabout had never been made for a Silver Ghost, the body was built directly on the chassis. The first boards were laid, the bolts put through, and the heads buried in the rest of the framing. The Springfield factory was still in preproduction in 1921, and this was one of the first cars to be completed. The American branch would continue to build Rolls-Royce models in the United States until the Great Depression took its toll on sales and Springfield ceased production in 1934.

The magnificent Springfield coachwork on this car was accented by what might appear to be the liberal use of chrome plating throughout the interior and on the body, but because chrome had not yet been applied to automobile finishes in 1921, it was all German silver and nickel plating!

A total of 79 runabouts, or Piccadilly Roadsters, were produced on the Silver Ghost chassis after 1921 and another 50 on the later Springfield Phantom I chassis, all of which were built in the United States. The 1921 Springfield runabout is the first and the rarest of the great Piccadilly Roadsters.

Owned today by noted Rolls-Royce collectors Tom and Abby Campi and restored to its original fit and finish, the runabout is regarded as the finest example of the 1921 Springfield Rolls in America and one of automotive history's truly great cars.

Rolls-Royce

Phantom II Brewster Town Car

Messrs. Charles Rolls and Henry Royce had a penchant for haunting names, and the first Rolls-Royce models, bearing the spiritual appellation "Silver Ghost," gave way in 1925 to a new model known as the Phantom. Essentially an improved version of the Silver Ghost, equipped with a more powerful six-cylinder engine, the Phantom became something of a transitional model, being built for only four years—for Rolls-Royce, a relatively short model run, considering that the Silver Ghost had been produced from 1907 to 1925!

The next evolution of the design came with the Phantom II, introduced in September 1929. A thoroughly modern car with improved suspension and chassis, four-speed transmission, and a resounding 158 horsepower six-cylinder engine beneath the far-reaching hood, the PII received numerous changes during its six-year production run as Rolls-Royce continued to keep pace with the ever-changing automotive industry of the 1930s.

One of the best engineered and most reliable cars of its time, the Phantom II is best remembered for the striking array of handcrafted coachwork that graced the 144-inch short wheelbase and 150-inch long wheelbase chassis. A total of 1,767 Phantom IIs were produced through 1935, one of the most spectacular of which was this regal long wheelbase town car bodied in the United States by New York City coachbuilder Brewster & Co. This was the second body on the 1930 Phantom II chassis, which was purchased by film star Constance Bennett in 1936.

The original sales card from J. S. Inskip, the New York sales office for Rolls-Royce, shows the car having been originally sold with a Trouville body in 1931 and traded back in 1935, after which it was rebodied by Brewster for the 1936 New York Auto Show.

The Brewster is one of the most striking town cars of the 1930s, with a rakish V-windshield, luxurious interior appointments, and highly detailed, hand-painted cane work along the body, which became a hallmark of the New York City coachbuilder.

Bennett saw the car at the auto show, purchased it from Inskip for $17,000, and had the three-ton Rolls-Royce shipped to her Holmby Hills estate in Los Angeles. A pretty hefty sum for a secondhand car, the intrepid actress earned back all of the money she paid by renting the Phantom to the movie studios for $250 a day!

Because of its elegant, one-of-a-kind Art Deco styling, Bennett's car appeared in a number of MGM films, including the 1937 classic *The King and the Chorus Girl* starring Fernand Gravet, Jane Wyman, Edward Everett Horton, and Joan Blondell. "For its acting services," wrote Bennett to later owner William Young in 1961, "it was a standing joke in Hollywood that the car received more salary than many players. It was in a picture once with Carol Lombard for three weeks."

Bennett kept the car for more than a decade, until her husband lost it in a poker game in 1948. Young sold the Phantom to J. B. Nethercutt in January 1985. Restored to its original glamour, it is one of the signature cars on exhibit at the renowned Nethercutt Collection.

1930 ROLLS-ROYCE PHANTOM II BREWSTER TOWN CAR

Stutz DV–32

LeBaron Sedan

Stutz was a leader, not a follower, of trends, a company that committed more of its resources to engineering and development than almost any independent automaker of its time. The Indianapolis, Indiana, firm, founded in 1911 by Harry C. Stutz, backed up its claims of building the safest cars in America with features such as the Stutz Side Bumper, comprising of steel running boards integrated with the frame for added protection in side-impact collisions and Stutz shatterproof safety glass, used for the windshield, side door glass, and even windwings. Stutz pioneered an industry standard with shatterproof glass that would eventually be adopted by every automaker in the world.

The final evolution of the Safety Stutz arrived in 1931 with the DV–32, a massive car spurred by a 156-horsepower, 32-valve (four valves per cylinder), double overhead camshaft straight eight. The DV–32 engine was a dramatically new design, regarded as much for what it did not have as for what it did. For example, it did not have a fan belt. The fan was mounted directly on a shaft operated from the timing chain, which was used in place of traditional timing gears, and the camshaft in the Stutz engine controlled valve actuation without the use of rocker arms, pushrods, or rollers!

Built on a 145-inch-wheelbase chassis, the DV–32s were long enough to allow virtually any type of body to fit from a formal sedan, such as the elegant 1931 LeBaron model pictured from the Nethercutt Collection, to a sporty dual windshield Speedster Phaeton.

Unfortunately for Stutz, the DV–32 arrived at a most inopportune time in American history, just as the Great Depression was gathering momentum and new car sales were plummeting. Despite being one of the most innovative automobiles of its time, fewer than 1,500 Stutz models were sold throughout the early 1930s, and after sales plunged to just six cars, Stutz ended automobile production in 1934.

Talbot-Lago
T150 SS Teardrop Coupé

Many of the body designs produced by France's most respected *carrosserie* in the 1930s might have appeared outrageous, designed for the solitary purpose of attracting attention, but the innovative French designers were attempting to do something more than simply turn heads along the Champs Elysées. The cars bodied by stylists such as Joseph Figoni in the 1930s and 1940s were also serious studies in the field of aerodynamics.

In the late 1920s, the French developed an aerodynamic design principle known as *goutte d'eau*, literally translated, "a drop of water"—nature's perfect aerodynamic shape. It gave the obsequious fenderlines of French cars new prominence and lent itself to bold, sweeping coachwork.

The masters of *goutte d'eau* design, Joseph Figoni and his associate Ovidio Falaschi, awed and often shocked the automotive world of the 1930s with extraordinary designs. *Goutte d'eau* was the inspiration for nearly all of Figoni's unorthodox but often beautiful body styles produced for Bugatti, Delahaye, Delage, and Talbot-Lago. The most dramatic of these were the Talbot-Lago T150 SS Coupés. No more than a dozen were built.

The teaming of Joseph Figoni with automaker Major Anthony Lago, who snatched Talbot from the brink of insolvency in 1934, was perhaps the most profound success story of the era. Lago stepped in with his own money to purchase the insolvent Automobiles Talbot and Société

Anonyme Darracq, literally rebuilding it from the ground up in just five years. He did this by producing sporty road cars that could also double as race cars.

Although the workers at the Talbot factory in Suresnes thought this was an odd way to bring vitality back into the financially bereft company, by 1937 Talbot-Lago sports cars were defeating the leading European marques, finishing first, second, third, and fifth in the French Grand Prix (later known as the 24 Hours of LeMans), winning the famed Tourist Trophy, and taking the checkered flag in both the Marseilles and Tunis Grands Prix. By 1938, the company was one of the three top contenders in French motorsports.

The T150 SS was a far more complicated design than many realized at the time of its introduction in the late 1930s. As with most Figoni coachwork, the power of the body was gathered around the wheels, which were enclosed in thin, flowing, independent teardrop fender pods separate from the body but blended to look like an integral part of it. The doors were another masterpiece, large rear-hinged ovals that opened away from the body, allowing easier entry and exit from the egg-shaped passenger compartment. The teardrop body design actually served to elongate the car's appearance, because the T150 SS had a relatively short wheelbase.

This graceful, plum-colored Lago Special, one of only a handful built with aerodynamic concealed headlights recessed into the fenders, is from the Peter Mullin Collection and is regarded as the finest example of the T150 SS in the world.

Volkswagen Beetle

Although Dr. Ferdinand Porsche is generally given credit for Adolf Hitler's Volkswagen, the car actually had many fathers. And not enough mothers to produce even one for sale to the Volk.

Because the *führer* of the German people, from 1933 to the bitter end in 1945, never learned to drive, his idea of a cheap automobile for the Teutonic mob that was to rule the world had the purity of the unreal. After all, if your dream of a cheap car for the Master Race barks your shin when you try to shift gears, there is a sudden reintroduction to reality.

Would the VW have been a decent car for the masses in the late 1930s? By the standards of the day (deep, worldwide economic depression, when the working class didn't have automobiles), probably. It was supposed to be priced at DM 1,000 (about U.S. $250.00). Even a guy with a job flipping Weiner schnitzel ought to have been able to raise that.

In 1938, the factory foundation was laid. In 1939, the Stuttgart shop of Dr. Ferdinand Porsche created three VW race cars for the Berlin-Rome race, canceled because Germany invaded Poland on September 1.

During the unpleasantries, the VW works built the Kubelwagen and the four-wheel-drive amphibious vehicles that went to Russia and never came back. When the madness ended and the smoke cleared, the four-power occupation of the once-mighty Third Reich found Great Britain in charge of the real estate upon which the once hoped for People's Car Works remained, some parts still warm to the touch.

The British military (a tidy bunch) immediately began to seek automobile manufacturers to come and get the factory up and running so the occupation forces could have some cars to scoot around in like real visitors. The English motor industry movers and shakers came and went, after giving the factory remains the once-over and leaving notes that mostly started with "You must be joking . . ."

Henry Ford II came, looked, and said something even less refined.

The occupiers finally caught on, and it became obvious that, if the German VW Works was to be revived, it would be the German workers who would revive it.

The first cars (such as this handsomely restored example from the Nethercutt Collection in a typical postwar paint scheme) weren't all that slick (at least by U.S. standards), but they sure beat walking.

In the fullness of time, the little rear-engine, air-cooled VW Beetle improved greatly; an American advertising agency put together a campaign that is still taught to marketing scholars; the Beetle began to be built far from Wolfsburg (as far as South America), to be driven by people who couldn't point to Germany on a map; Henry Ford's 20-million-car sales record for the Model T was eclipsed; and the VW came to be so loved that, a generation after the last one was built, Volkswagen has introduced a VW Beetle for the twenty-first century. In this one instance, history has repeated itself, all for the better.

1946 VOLKSWAGEN BEETLE

A P P E N D I X

101.	1956 AC Bristol (Ace)	135.	1931 Duesenberg Model SJ Weymann/Bohman &	168.	1963 Mercedes-Benz 600
102.	1972 Alfa Romeo Montreal		Schwartz Mudd Coupe	169.	1965 Mercedes-Benz 600 Landaulet
103.	1950 Allard J2	136.	1956 Facel Vega	170.	1968 Mercedes-Benz 300SEL 6.3
104.	1982 Aston-Martin Lagonda	137.	1949 Ferrari 166 Convertible	171.	1928 Minerva
105.	1963 Aston-Martin DB 5	138.	1956 Ferrari 410 Super America	172.	1904 Packard Touring
106.	1964 Austin Healey 3000 Mk III	139.	1975 Ferrari 308 GTB	173.	1909 Packard Model 18 Runabout
107.	1963 Austin Mini Cooper S	140.	1988 Ferrari F40	174.	1932 Packard Twin Six Convertible Coupe
108.	1932 Austro Daimler	141.	1996 Ferrari F50	175.	1934 Packard Dual Cowl Phaeton
109.	1923 Avions Voison	142.	1998 Ferrari 550 Maranello	176.	1934 Packard 1106 Sport Coupe
110.	1972 BMW 2002 Tii Coupe	143.	1954 Fiat Otto Vu	177.	1955–56 Packard Caribbean
111.	1930 Bugatti Royale	144.	1932 Ford V-8	178.	1910 Pierce-Arrow
112.	1948 Buick Roadmaster	145.	1957 Ford Fairlane Retractable	179.	1970 Plymouth Hemi 'Cuda
113.	1954 Buick Skylark	146.	1955 Jaguar D-Type	180.	1970 Plymouth Superbird/Dodge Daytona
114.	1939 Cadillac Sixty Special	147.	1954 Jaguar XK–140MC Roadster	181.	1956 Pontiac Star Chief Convertible
115.	1957 Cadillac Eldorado Biarritz	148.	1958 Jaguar XK–150S 3.4 Roadster	182.	1967 Pontiac GTO
116.	1958 Cadillac Sixty Special	149.	1966–1972 Jensen Interceptor FF	183.	1911 Pope Hartford
117.	1955 Chevrolet Bel Air	150.	1937 Lagonda LG–45 Rapide	184.	1952 Porsche America
118.	1955 Chevrolet Corvette V-8	151.	1968 Lamborghini Espada	185.	1954 Porsche 356 Coupe
119.	1967 Chevrolet Camaro	152.	1974–78 Lamborghini Countach LP400	186.	1955 Porsche 550 Spyder
120.	1969 Chevrolet Corvette L–88	153.	1994 Lamborghini Diablo VT	187.	1964 Porsche 904 Carrera GTS
121.	1963 Citroën 2CV	154.	1932 Lancia DeLambda	188.	1967 Porsche 911S Targa
122.	1970 Citroën SM Maserati	155.	1954 Lancia B24 S Spyder	189.	1987–92 Porsche 928S–4
123.	1990 Chevrolet Corvette ZR–1	156.	1925 Locomobile	190.	1923 Renault Model 45
124.	1924 Chrysler Imperial	157.	1957 Lotus 7	191.	1930 Rolls-Royce Phantom I
125.	1932 Chrysler Speedster	158.	1958 Lotus Elite	192.	1937 Rolls-Royce Phantom III
126.	1934 Chrysler Airflow	159.	1962 Lotus Elan S1 Convertible	193.	1909 Stanley Steamer
127.	1957 Chrysler 300C	160.	1932 Marmon V-16	194.	1956 Studebaker Golden Hawk
128.	1902 De Dion Buton	161.	1957 Maserati A6G 2000	195.	1963 Studebaker Avanti
129.	1968 DeTomaso Mangusta	162.	1969 Maserati Ghibli SS Spyder	196.	1966 Triumph GT–6+
130.	1971 DeTomaso Pantera	163.	1979 Maserati Quattroporte II	197.	1967 Triumph TR–4A
131.	1925 Doble Series E Steam Car	164.	1935 Mercedes-Benz 500K Sport Roadster	198.	1968 Triumph TR–250
132.	1998 Dodge Viper GTS	165.	1954 Mercedes-Benz 190SL	199.	1969 Triumph TR–6
133.	1956 Dual Ghia	166.	1959 Mercedes-Benz 220 SE Cabriolet	200.	1948 Tucker
134.	1924 Duesenberg Model A	167.	1968 Mercedes-Benz 280SL		

BIBLIOGRAPHY

BY DENNIS ADLER

Standard Catalog of American Cars, 1805–1942, by Beverly Rae Kimes and Henry Austin Clark Jr., 1985, Krause Publications, Iola, Wisconsin.

Collector Cars by Lee Culpepper, 1989, Octopus Books, London.

The Illustrated Encyclopedia of the World's Automobiles, by David Burgess Wise, 1979, Quarto Publishing, Chartwell Books, London.

The World Guide to Automobile Manufacturers, by Nick Baldwin, G.N. Georgano, Michael Sedgwick, and Brian Laban, 1987, MacDonald & Co., London.

100 Years of the World's Automobiles, 1962, G. N. Georgano, Floyd Clymer Publications, North Hollywood, California.

Automobile and Culture, by Gerald Silk, Henry Flood Robert, Jr., Strother MacMinn, and Angelo Tito Anselmi, 1984, Harry N. Abrams, New York.

Packard—A History of the Motor Car and the Company, Beverly Rae Kimes, editor, 1978, Automobile Quarterly Publications. kutztown, Pennsylvania

80 Years of Cadillac LaSalle, by Walter M.P. McCall, 1982, Crestline Publishing, Sarasota, Florida.

The Marmon Heritage by George Philip Hanley and Stacey Hanley, 1985, Doyle Hyk Publishing, Rochester, Michigan.

Marmon—The History of a Success, 1916, Marmon Sales Extension Division, Indianapolis, Indiana.

Pace Cars of the Indy 500, by L. Spencer Riggs, Speed Age.

The Marmon Post, 1920, The Hollenbeck Press.

Automobile Trade Journal, August 20, 1920.

The Ferrari Legend, by Antoine Prunet, 1981, E.P.A. Editions, Paris, France.

Ferrari, by Hans Tanner and Doug Nye, 1984, Haynes Publishing Group, England.

Illustrated Ferrari Buyers Guide, by Dean Batchelor, 1981, Motorbooks International, Osceola, Wisconsin.

Un Siecle de Carrosserie Francaise by Jean-Henri Labourdette, published in French by Edita in 1972. Our special thanks to bookseller T. E. Warth and translator Lisa Seiffert, Paris, France.

Auburn, Cord, Duesenberg, by Don Butler, 1992, Motorbooks International.

The Cars of Lincoln Mercury, by Geo. H. Dammann and James K. Wagner, 1987, Crestline Publishing, Sarasota, Florida.

Duesenberg: The Mightiest American Motor Car, by J. L. Elbert, 1975, Post-Era Books, Arcadia, California.

Mercedes-Benz 300SL, by Dennis Adler, 1994, Motorbooks International, Osceola, Wisconsin.

Mercedes-Benz: 110 Years of Excellence, by Dennis Adler, 1995, Motorbooks International, Osceola, Wisconsin.

Fifties Flashback—The American Car, by Dennis Adler, 1996, Motorbooks International, Osceola, Wisconsin.

Speed & Luxury—The Great Cars, by Dennis Adler, 1997, Motorbooks International, Osceola, Wisconsin.

Ferrari, by Dennis Adler, 1997, Motorbooks International, Osceola, Wisconsin.

Packard, by Dennis Adler, 1998, Motorbooks International, Osceola, Wisconsin.

Corvettes—The Cars That Created the Legend, by Dennis Adler, 1996, Krause Publications, Iola, Wisconsin.

The Cars of San Sylmar—The Nethercutt Collection, by Dennis Adler, 1999, Blue Book Publications, Minneapolis, Minnesota, and The Nethercutt Collection.

Additional information provided by T. C. Browne, the Indianapolis Motor Speedway Museum, Chrysler Corporation, Daimler-Benz AG, (DaimlerChrysler), Porsche AG, and Ferrari S.p.A.